CONTENTS

Ships in Focus Publications

Correspondence and editorial:
Roy Fenton
18 Durrington Avenue, London SW20 8NT
020 8879 3527
rfenton@rfenton.demon.co.uk

Orders and photographic:
John & Marion Clarkson
18 Franklands, Longton, Preston PR4 5PD
01772 612855
sales@shipsinfocus.co.uk
© 2003 Individual contributors, John Clarkson and Roy Fenton.

Printed by Amadeus Press Ltd., Cleckheaton, Yorkshire.
Designed by Hugh Smallwood, John Clarkson and Roy Fenton.
SHIPS IN FOCUS RECORD
ISBN 1 901703 71-1

SHIPS IN FOCUS
Septembe

With a new volume of *Record*, we are making a change subscription offered to readers. Subscriptions are essential to a specialist journal like this, which could not sustain - and does not want - news-stand sales. Subscriptions and the equally welcome advanced orders allow us to set the print run, and give us some certainty that what we produce is likely to sell. To encourage subscribers, we have made long-term offers: up to nine issues, at favourable rates. However, we now feel it is advisable to limit future subscriptions to three or four issues. This is due to uncertainty about future postal rates, and to concerns that EC pressure may persuade the British Government to put VAT on postage and books. Those who only send letters at the basic first- and second-class rates may not have realised that higher postal rates have increased much more rapidly in recent years. With the prospect of these rises continuing, and the possibility of VAT being imposed, we feel we cannot give long-term commitments about subscription rates. The three and four issue rates are listed below. We hardly need to add that existing long-term subscriptions will be fully honoured.

Even for three or four issues, subscriptions give big advantages to readers, including savings over buying copies individually, plus significant discounts on other Ships in Focus publications. Indeed, we have a very full programme of books planned, with at least four substantial hardbacks due in the next 12 months, all of which will be available to subscribers at a reduced cost.

We are very keen to increase the number of our subscribers. If any readers have friends or colleagues who they think might like to subscribe, please let us know their name and postal address, and we will send them a free copy of an earlier edition, with subscription details. So, if you don't already subscribe, discover for yourself the savings and convenience of a three or four-issue sub, and tell your friends about it, too.

John Clarkson   Roy Fenton

SUBSCRIPTION RATES FOR RECORD

Readers can start their subscription with any issue, and are welcome to backdate it to receive previous issues.

	3 issues	4 issues
UK	£23	£32
Europe (airmail)	£25	£34
Rest of world (surface mail)	£25	£34
Rest of world (airmail)	£30	£40

Canadian Pacific's *Beaverdale*. See page 4. *[J. and M. Clarkson]*

Beaverford on the Scheldt. See page 4. *[World Ship Photo Library]*

CANADIAN PACIFIC'S BEAVERS: Part 1
Stephen Howells

When Shaw, Savill introduced the passenger-only *Southern Cross* on their Australian service in 1955, much was made of the 'innovation' of separating passenger and cargo carrying (see 'Shaw, Savill's Big Ics' in *Record* 24 for instance). Yet, such a partition had been the norm on North Atlantic services for many years. Canadian Pacific were notable in building a dedicated fleet of cargo liners in the 1920s. As first and foremost a railway company, Canadian Pacific could readily offer shippers through services from and to inland Canadian destinations, with rail to ship transfer facilities at Montreal, Quebec City and St. John. However, they did not fully exploit this position until the five 'Beavers' delivered in 1927 and 1928 allowed them to offer regular sailings from Europe to Canada.

Canadian Pacific and the Atlantic
The Canadian Pacific Railway Company was incorporated in 1881 in order to build a railway which would, it was hoped, turn the confederation of British-ruled provinces in North America into a nation. The promise of such a transcontinental railway had been used to help persuade British Columbia to join the confederation, the Dominion of Canada, in 1871. From early in its inception, the railway was seen as important for Britain's imperial interests, linking steamship routes across the Atlantic and Pacific and offering a faster service to the far east and Australasia. Canadian Pacific were not slow to involve themselves with ocean-going steamships, chartering three former Cunard ships for a Pacific service until their first three 'Empresses' were delivered in 1890 and 1891.

The railway was much slower to develop its transatlantic services, partly because existing lines were well entrenched - especially on routes to the USA - and partly because the St. Lawrence was ice-bound in winter, closing Montreal, Canada's main east coast port. The formation in 1902 of the US-controlled International Mercantile Marine (IMM) worried the British and Canadian Governments, who assumed the IMM's routes to the United States would come to dominate transatlantic services. In response to the British Government giving subsidies to Cunard to help them compete, the Canadian Government offered a mail contract to help Canadian Pacific begin its own services in winter. As a result, Canadian Pacific - now financially strong - bought Elder, Dempster's Beaver Line with its eight passenger and seven cargo ships operating a service from Bristol and Liverpool to Montreal using St. John, New Brunswick or Halifax in winter. The Beaver Line ships were not fast, and Canadian Pacific were well aware that better ships were needed to compete, especially with the Allan Line (who were, in fact, to be taken over secretly by Canadian Pacific in 1909). The first priority was passenger ships, and fleet renewal began in 1906 with the delivery of the 18-knot *Empress of Britain*. Cargo ships were a lesser priority, and mostly second-hand vessels were bought to supplement the existing ships and to replace losses during the First World War.

The first Beavers
Canadian Pacific's vision of a uniform fleet of fast cargo liners to handle Canada's growing trade was realised in 1928 with the completion of an order for five exceptionally well-equipped ships designed by Denny. They were given 'Beaver' names in commemoration of the Beaver Line. The Beavers were intended to maintain a sea speed of 14 knots on the North Atlantic throughout the year, and to do this were given two Parsons turbines driving twin screws. These

were fed with steam superheated to 250 degrees by four Yarrow water tube boilers. They were coal fired, but an important innovation was the use of Erith-Roe mechanical stokers, a type not used previously at sea but well tried in power stations. Besides reducing the need for firemen, mechanical stoking improved efficiency. It meant it was easier to achieve an even rate of firing which maintained optimal steam pressure, whilst mechanical removal of ash eliminated the need to interrupt stoking to remove it manually. The first, the Denny-built *Beaverburn*, achieved a speed of just over 15 knots on trials

Cargo facilities included six holds, some with deep tanks, providing 570,000 cubic feet of space plus 80,000 cubic feet of insulated space for meat. Four of the lower holds were ventilated to carry apples, whilst the holds could be used for grain, and cattle could be accommodated in portable stalls in the 'tween decks. To handle cargo, 27 derricks were provided. With their four goalpost masts plus two sets of kingposts they were very reminiscent of the slightly smaller Furness 'London' ships of six years before (featured in *Record* 17), especially in carrying topmasts on the first and fourth goalposts. However, the Canadian Pacific ships were significantly cheaper, *Beaverburn* costing £262,823 compared with the £458,598 for each of the Furness ships, illustrating how shipbuilding prices had fallen during the depressed 1920s.

The accommodation in the 'Beavers' for 12 passengers plus 79 officers and crew was all placed amidships. The ships were ice strengthened. Colour scheme was black hull with green boot-topping, and plain yellow funnel.

The arrival of the 'Beavers' allowed the older ships to be disposed of. Cargo services were now concentrated on London, Antwerp, Hamburg and Le Havre, although occasional calls were made at Avonmouth, Glasgow, Southampton and Liverpool. The five new ships meant one could leave Montreal every Friday and be ready to discharge in Surrey Docks, London the second following Monday. The fleet made on average fifty round voyages annually, with St. John the terminal port in winter when Montreal was ice bound. Speed and regularity, plus good rail connections in Canada, were necessary to compete on the North Atlantic.

The turboelectric Beavers
The Second World War was disastrous for the five 'Beavers', four being sunk through enemy action and the fifth lost through a rather trivial accident at St. John. The early war losses were undoubtedly factors in the company being allowed to order four new cargo liners in 1943, although none were delivered until the war was over. Company staff had drawn up their specification, appropriately, in an air raid shelter. They were originally to have geared turbines, but lack of gear-cutting capacity meant that turbo-electric machinery was specified instead, a relative rarity in British cargo vessels. The turbo-alternators were supplied by Parsons, but this time were fed with steam at 850 degrees Fahrenheit and 850 psi from a single oil-fired water-tube boiler.

Compared with their predecessors, these Beavers were slightly shorter, had a crew reduced to 64, but had enhanced capacity for refrigerated cargo. This was not to be used to its full potential, as Canadian meat exports did not come up to expectations in post-war years. The new design continued to use goalpost masts, with four ahead of the superstructure and two aft.
To be continued.

BEAVERBURN (1) (top)

William Denny and Brothers Ltd., Dumbarton, 1927, 9,874g 503 feet
Two three-stage Parsons-type steam turbines by William Denny and Brothers Ltd., Dumbarton; 8,000 SHP.
Although Dennys designed the original 'Beavers', they built only the *Beaverburn*, other yards being given contracts in order to expedite the entry into service of the five ships. *Beaverburn* was the first, launched on 27th September 1927 and leaving on her maiden voyage from Glasgow on Christmas Eve.

Beaverburn was also the first of the five to be lost. She left London for Canada on 1st February 1940 to join convoy OB 84. Just after 13.00 hours on 5th February, in position 49.20 north by 10.07 west, *Beaverburn* was struck by a torpedo fired by *U 41*. Hit right amidships, she quickly began to break in two, and sank only nine minutes after the torpedo struck. Yet, losses were extremely light, only the chief cook who returned to his room after reaching his boat station. Seventy six survivors were rescued by the US tanker *Narraganset*. Revenge was to be swift: the convoy's lone escort, the destroyer HMS *Antelope*, fixed *U 41* with her sonar, depth charged and destroyed the submarine and her crew. *[George Scott collection]*

BEAVERFORD (1) (middle)

Barclay Curle and Co. Ltd., Whiteinch, Glasgow; 1928, 10,042gt, 503 feet
Two three-stage steam turbines by Parsons Marine Steam Turbine Co. Ltd., Newcastle-upon-Tyne; 8,000 SHP.
Dennys supplied guidance plans to Barclay, Curle to build their pair of 'Beavers', of which *Beaverford* was launched in October 1927 and delivered in time to make her maiden voyage from Glasgow on 21st January 1928.

Beaverford was to become a war hero. On 5th October 1940 she was eastbound from Halifax when her convoy HX 84 was sighted by a reconnaissance aircraft from the German *Panzerschiff Admiral Scheer*, which had been alerted to the sailing of the convoy probably by signal's intelligence from the Kriegsmarine B Dienst. The convoy's sole escort, the armed merchant cruiser HMS *Jervis Bay*, signalled the convoy to scatter and - to give time for them to escape - engaged her far mightier adversary for almost an hour before being sunk. When the *Admiral Scheer* pursued the other ships of the convoy, *Beaverford* turned to fight. Although armed with only one four-inch and one three-inch gun, she engaged the enemy for four to five hours, according to one account, aided by the *Admiral Scheer's* cautious tactics, before *Beaverford* was torpedoed and blew up with the loss of all on board. As a result, most of the convoy escaped into the darkness, and losses were much lighter than might have been expected. *[Roy Fenton collection]*

BEAVERDALE (1) (above and opposite top)

Sir W.G. Armstrong, Whitworth and Co. Ltd., Newcastle-upon-Tyne; 1928, 9,957gt, 502 feet
Two three-stage steam turbines by Parsons Marine Steam Turbine Co. Ltd., Newcastle-upon-Tyne; 8,000 SHP.
Launched just one day after *Beaverburn*, *Beaverdale* was completed more slowly, and left the Tyne on her maiden voyage to St. John, New Brunswick, via Antwerp on 1st February 1928.

In May 1933, *Beaverdale* sailed from London for Montreal with LMS locomotive No. 6100 *Royal Scot* and eight coaches from the train which was also named *Royal Scot* which made an eight-month promotional tour of Canada and the USA. Photographs exist of her arriving at Montreal with the train as deck cargo and the editors would be pleased to hear from any reader who can locate a source of a print.

Beaverdale's war story was to be an adventurous if ultimately tragic one. Like the other 'Beavers', she came under Government control early in the war, and in September and October 1939 made voyages from Liverpool and Avonmouth into the River Loire with small quantities of Government cargo. She was docked in London in late May 1940, and her chief officer took two of her lifeboats across to Dunkirk to aid in the evacuation, returning safely. Her end came on 1st April 1941. In the early hours of the morning she was torpedoed by the German submarine *U 48* in the North Atlantic in position 60.50 north by 29.19 west. The crew of 79 had time to take to the three boats before the submarine surfaced to finish off the *Beaverdale* with gunfire. It is possible that one of the ship's boats was also sunk at the time, as only two managed to reach safety, one getting to Iceland and the other being picked up by an Icelandic trawler.

According to one account, *Beaverdale* was in convoy SC 26 at the time of her sinking. However, 'The Allied Convoy System' by Arnold Hague does not list her as one of the several ships sunk from this convoy, and the nature of the attack makes it much more likely that she was proceeding alone. As a 14-knot ship, *Beaverdale* would not be consigned to a slow convoy like SC 26. *[Both: Roy Fenton collection]*

BEAVERHILL (1) (middle and bottom)

Barclay Curle and Co. Ltd., Glasgow; 1928, 10,041gt, 503 feet

Two three-stage steam turbines by Parsons Marine Steam Turbine Co. Ltd., Newcastle-upon-Tyne; 8,000 SHP.

During the Second World War, *Beaverhill* was regarded as a lucky ship, as during 55 wartime crossings of the North Atlantic she was not bothered by enemy action. In 1941 she was fitted with additional accommodation in her 'tween decks and holds for 138 passengers in order to carry RAF aircrew to and from their training in Canada. *Beaverhill* carried extra boats for this enhanced complement, as seen in the accompanying 1943 photograph of her in convoy HXM 292.

Her luck ran out on 24th November 1944. Whilst in the harbour at St. John, New Brunswick a towing hawser broke and tangled round one of her propellers. Wind and tide set her on to Hillyards Reef and she broke her back as the tide receded. In December 1946 the stern section was refloated and towed back to St. John. It later sank at its berth, but was refloated once again. Repairs were estimated at a prohibitive $1.3 million dollars, so the remains of *Beaverhill* were towed out to sea to be scuttled off Grand Manan Island. *[World Ship Photo Library and P. Ransome-Wallis]*

BEAVERBRAE (1) (both above)
Sir W.G. Armstrong, Whitworth and Co. Ltd., Newcastle-upon-Tyne; 1928, 9,956g, 502 feet
Two three-stage steam turbines by Parsons Marine Steam Turbine Co. Ltd., Newcastle-upon-Tyne; 8,000 SHP.
The first five 'Beavers' escaped only mining in the Second World War, being sunk by submarine, by surface raiders, by marine hazards, and by air attack in case of the *Beaverbrae*. On 25th March 1941 she was attacked in position 60.12 north by 09.00 west by a Focke Wulf Fw200, whose first bombing run scored direct hits on her after deck. During the second and third runs the pilot seems to have been distracted by gunfire from *Beaverbrae*, but strafing caused some casualties. However, the fires caused could not be brought under control, and *Beaverbrae* was abandoned, the entire crew being rescued from their boats by destroyers which arrived about 12 hours later. *[Both: Roy Fenton collection]*

BEAVERDELL (opposite top) and **MAPLEDELL** (opposite middle)
Lithgows Ltd., Port Glasgow; 1946, 9,901gt, 498 feet
Two steam turbines by C.A. Parsons and Co. Ltd., Newcastle-upon-Tyne connected to electric motors.
First of the war-designed 'Beavers' was launched on 27th August 1945 and entered service in February 1946.

    Beaverdell and her sister *Beavercove* were transferred to Pacific services in August 1952, running from Vancouver to Cebu, Manila, Kobe and Yokohama. *Beaverdell* became *Mapledell*, but the service did not prosper, and she was returned to the Atlantic in June 1954, although she did not regain her original name until December 1956.

    In January 1963, *Beaverdell* was sold to the Genoa-based Costa company, becoming *Luisa Costa* (see also page 9). She survived until March 1971 when she arrived at La Spezia to be broken up. *[Roy Fenton collection and World Ship Photo Library]*

BEAVERGLEN (opposite bottom)
Lithgows Ltd., Port Glasgow; 1946, 9,824gt, 498 feet
Two steam turbines by C.A. Parsons and Co. Ltd., Newcastle-upon-Tyne connected to electric motors.
Post-war, Canadian Pacific painted its houseflag on the ships' funnels. The red and white chequers represented the maps showing plots of land alongside the railway, sale of which helped fund its construction.

    In September 1963, *Beaverglen* was renamed *Bermuda Hibiscus* when sold to Hibiscus Ltd. of Hamilton, Bermuda, a rather anonymous company which seems not to have owned any other ships. In April 1965 the ship was resold to Teh-Hu Steamship Co. (Hong Kong) Ltd. and renamed *Ping An*, but was to have only a short further life. On 24th November 1965 *Ping An* stranded near Terheidan, five miles north of the Hook of Holland, when her engine failed and her anchor chains parted in heavy weather. The wreck was sold to H.P. Heuvelman N.V. for breaking up. *[J. and M. Clarkson]*

BEAVERLAKE (middle)
Lithgows Ltd., Port Glasgow; 1946, 9,824gt, 498 feet
Two steam turbines by C.A. Parsons and Co. Ltd., Newcastle-upon-Tyne connected to electric motors.
At the end of her Canadian Pacific career in June 1952, *Beaverlake* went with two sisters to the Italian Costa company, who registered her in the ownership of Lloyd Tirrenico SpA, Genoa, Italy as *Bice Costa*. She arrived at La Spezia for breaking up in April 1971. *[A. Duncan]*

BEAVERCOVE (bottom),
MAPLECOVE (opposite top) and
GIOVANNO COSTA (opposite middle)
Fairfield Shipbuilding and Engineering Co. Ltd., Govan; 1947, 9,824gt, 498 feet
Two steam turbines by C.A. Parsons and Co. Ltd., Newcastle-upon-Tyne connected to electric motors.
Beavercove was transferred to Pacific services as *Maplecove* in August 1952, but it was to be an unfortunate chapter in her career. Not only did trade not develop as anticipated, but on her second voyage across the Pacific in December 1952 *Maplecove* lost part of her stern in a storm, and had to be rescued by the tug *Island Sovereign* and returned to Vancouver. Back on the Atlantic by July 1954, she retained the name *Maplecove* until December 1956.

In August 1963 she was sold to Giacomo Costa fu Andrea of Genoa and served as *Giovanna Costa* until broken up at La Spezia in March 1971. *[Roy Fenton collection, F.R. Sherlock]*

Another look at a Beaver in Costa colours, the *Luisa Costa*, ex *Beaverdell*, at Las Palmas in 1968. The photograph emphasises her powerful appearance; a ship quite capable of taking on the North Atlantic in winter. Viewed from this angle, her funnel looks particularly massive, and reference to the photographs on page 7 suggests that her funnel was larger than her sister *Beaverglen*.

[Peter Newall collection]

To be continued

Top: *Pass of Glenclunie* sailing from Preston in April 1967. *[J. and M. Clarkson]*

Middle: *Penelope Everard,* the largest ship on which Derick sailed. *[Charles Hill]*

Bottom: Everard's *Ability.* *[World Ship Photo Library]*

DERICK GOUBERT - CAPTAIN/OWNER
Ken Garrett

Derick James Goubert, a Guernseyman through and through, was born in 1947 and became interested in ships from a very early age. As a youngster, and probably to the detriment of his schooling, he spent all his spare time wandering around the harbour of St. Sampsons and gazing at the ships. During these visits he also got to know some of the crews and helped out doing odd jobs aboard. On a lucky day he would be invited aboard the pilot boat for a short trip.

One of the masters, Captain James Kelly of the tanker *Pass of Dalveen* (965/1958), offered him a job when he left school at the age of sixteen. But, before he could join the ship, Captain Kelly was transferred to the new *Pass of Glenclunie* (1,416/1963) then completing at Sunderland. Derick eventually joined and spent ten months on the ship. Always on the coast, he moved around and also sailed with Commodore Shipping Co. Ltd. and F.T. Everard and Sons Ltd.

After a few years his life settled into a pattern spending the winter months aboard an Everard or Commodore coaster and the summer on the little ferries plying between Guernsey and Herm. The largest ship he ever sailed on was the *Penelope Everard* (1,583/1963). Amongst other Everard ships, he sailed on the *Ability* (881/1943) and the *Scarcity* (586/1948). Also during this period he sailed with Alderney Shipping Co. Ltd. and was successively bosun, mate and master of the *Alderney Trader* (371/1952) and he also sailed as mate on the *Alderney Courier* (203/1940).

In 1973 while sailing with Commodore Shipping, mainly on the *Norman Commodore* (496/1971), he studied and passed the examination for his Mate's Home Trade certificate. He spent a while as mate of the *Commodore Clipper* (758/1970) on charter to the Guernsey Tomato Board. This was an idyllic trade for a Guernseyman because the ship sailed for Belfast on Monday and returned on Friday spending the weekend in his home port. Later, he went to the newer *Commodore Trader* (477/1971).

As something of a change he then went into more general coastwise ships and sailed on the *Wiggs* (199/1970) of Eggar, Forrester Ltd. and similar ships of Tower Shipping Ltd. for a while before returning to Alderney Shipping. Here he spent the next eight years in command of such ships as *Sea Trent* (200/1968), *La Pia* (398/1963) and *Courier* (290/1966).

Shipowning ambitions
But ambition was growing and after some discussion with John Churchward of Harris and Dixon (Shipbrokers) Ltd. in 1984, Derick agreed to take command of the *Finlandia* (399/1961) on the understanding that he would purchase the ship a year later. Harris and Dixon had bought the ship to satisfy the requirement to be trading in the current year to qualify for a loan for the new *Dowlais* (794/1985).

During the year Harris and Dixon carried out the freight management and R. Lapthorn and Sons Ltd. were the

technical managers. In preparation for the big event, Derick formed D.J. Goubert Shipping Ltd. in October 1985. Proceedings to purchase the vessel commenced in December 1985 and ship was registered in Guernsey and renamed *Mary Coast;* Mary being the name of his partner and the coast generally describing his intended area of operation. The management arrangements with Harris and Dixon and Lapthorns were continued. Much of his early work involved trips to Denmark and he named his house 'Thyboron' after the port at the western end of the Limfjord. After four years he decided that he needed a newer ship and set about selling the *Mary Coast.* The negotiations were prolonged and took eleven months to complete. As a complication, the ship was due for Special Survey and was laid up three times during the process. A Haitian buyer, based in the USA, was found and she was sold in March 1990.

Captain Derick Goubert. *[Author]*

Meanwhile, with thoughts of a time charter, Derick had been keeping an eye open for a suitable ship himself and had been discussing the purchase of the *Delce* (429/1971) with Whitbury Shipping Co. Ltd. who were disposing of their fleet. He bought the ship on 5th April 1990 and renamed her *Port Soif* after the place in Guernsey where he lived. By this time the Guernsey register for trading vessels had closed and the ship remained on the London register. Initially, Harris and Dixon carried out the freight management but the ship was soon taken on time charter by Alderney Shipping when the managers became Marine Services Ltd. of Guernsey. She not only carried general cargo from Torquay and Guernsey to Alderney but was also engaged in carrying bulk cargoes elsewhere. This mainly involved sand, aggregates and fertilisers on the south coast and Channel Islands, Fingringhoe, Weymouth, St. Malo and Guernsey. There were two memorable cargoes, for all the wrong reasons, of tar in barrels from Weymouth to Guernsey. Unfortunately the barrels leaked and the cargo left its mark in the hold. Under her new name she did not venture north of Harwich on the English coast but did once take a cargo of clay to Dordrecht followed by cattle feed to Ipswich.

A two-ship fleet
In the early 1990s, F.T. Everard and Sons Ltd. were considering the economics of small dry cargo ship operations and decided that as a high profile company they could not compete with the smaller companies and in particular the owner/master operation. They decided that they would sell off their fleet of six ships under 1,000 deadweight tons either by direct sale or by a mortgage. One of the attractions was the offer of the freight management expertise of Everard's well-established chartering department. Derick decided to take the *Candourity* (499/1975) and purchased the ship by way of a mortgage on 18th November 1992. He also signed a management agreement with Everards that tied him to their freight

Port Soif at Charlestown to load china clay.

[Derick Goubert collection]

management and also to retaining the ship's name, not that he had any particular name in mind. In any event he now had more than a ship's name to concern him. The problems associated with running a two-ship fleet are probably greater than the sum of the individual parts and in addition to the age-old problems of finding suitable crews, and the time and money for repairs and surveys, there now came all the new regulations from the International Maritime Organisation (IMO). These required new equipment and the writing of manuals on all manner of subjects, amongst them SOPEP, SOLAS, securing and garbage, and also the all embracing ISM Code.

The *Port Soif* and *Candourity* were both examples of a standard type of coaster built by various shipyards in the Dutch Conoship Group. Many were built for British owners from about 1969 until well into the 1970s. Although very similar in basic design, they were not a class as such; tonnages, dimensions, machinery and final outfit details varying according to the shipyard and the prospective owner's requirements.

Shortly after he took the ship, Derick had the hull colour changed from the Everard yellow to a more serviceable black and later to orange. The change of funnel colour has been an interesting sequence. As a first stage, the yellow was changed to the Goubert orange but the Everard flag was retained in the centre. There was no requirement for this but he considered that while the bulk of the mortgage was still outstanding the retention of the flag in some way declared the *status quo*. In much the same way as sailing ship men would celebrate the working off of advances of wages by throwing overboard the effigy of a dead horse, Derick celebrated the paying off of half the mortgage by painting up his own funnel motif. In actual fact, the two events did not precisely coincide because a jig saw was not available to cut out the 'G', but it was the original intention

The *Candourity* carried on trading much as she had in Everard days, so too the *Port Soif* carried on with her time charter to Alderney Shipping. She had an engine problem in 1991 and had to be re-engined with a similar unit. However, she had a major problem on 21st December 1993 when she struck the Amfroque Rock off Herm while on passage from

Upper: the funnel mark of *Candourity*, first stage. [Author]
Lower: The funnel mark of *Candourity*, second stage. [Author]

Alderney to Guernsey. She proceeded to St. Peter Port to discharge her cargo and then to St. Sampsons for slipping and survey. The damage was such that she was declared a constructive total loss and the insurance paid. The ship was later towed to Plymouth and then to Ramsgate where she was repaired, registered in Belize and with the name *Bahamas Provider* sailed for the Caribbean.

While the disposal of the *Port Soif* was taking place, Dennison Shipping Ltd. of Kirkwall was getting into terminal financial difficulties and ultimately went into

Lancresse (1) *[Derick Goubert collection]*

liquidation. Some of their ships were demise chartered from James Fisher and Sons PLC of Barrow-in-Furness and were repossessed and laid up for a short while in Birkenhead. Derick moved fast and purchased the *Bressay Sound* (664/1978) in April 1994. He commenced trading straightaway and did not stop to rename the ship until 3rd June 1994. The change of name to *Lancresse*, the part of Guernsey where he was brought up, was carried out in Leith. Despite the possibility of a Channel Island time charter he asked Everards to carry out the freight management which they were well qualified to do, having supervised the building and managed the ship from new as the *Edgar Dorman*. The Dennison red hull colour was soon overpainted with black.

Trading conditions were bad but not too bad in the early 1990s but when an offer was made for the *Lancresse* in 1996 it was very hard to refuse. A time charter had not materialised and the ship was sold to Unicorn Ltd., a subsidiary of Alderney Shipping. They renamed the ship *Burhou I* and she joined her sister ship *Isis*, formerly *Deer Sound* and *David Dorman,* in the Channel Islands trade.

A 'tween decker
Until now, all the Goubert ships had been single deck, gearless bulk carriers but Derick began to think that there might be richer pickings in the general and project cargo trades using a 'tween decker and ships gear. Such work has been carried out successfully by Danish ships for a number of years and eventually a ship for sale in Denmark was identified. The ship *Jenstar* (534/1975) was inspected and purchased in October 1997. She was renamed *Lancresse* and after some difficulties registered under the British flag. The hoped for cargoes did not materialise and for the most part she was engaged in the bulk trades for which she was not ideally suited. Ironically, one of the best project cargoes for which she was fixed was frustrated by strikes. By this time the coastal freight market had deteriorated to an alarming extent and a sale was negotiated to a Faroese company. They needed a geared 'tween decker to carry supplies for fish farms from Norway to the Faroes. She was sold in February 1999 and renamed *Skurin* by her new owner.

The *Candourity* was now left to carry on as the sole remaining ship. The freight market was generally bad and both owner and managers went from high to low again with the occasional false dawn. But even with a rare freight that could be described as good, there was precious little left at the end of the month. The only dependable operational aspect was the seemingly inevitable increase in costs. Bunkers, port charges, repairs and coping with the deluge of new regulations have all had a proportionately unfair effect on the smaller ships. Derick put the ship up for sale but, of course, freight and ship sale markets go in parallel and there were few enquiries or sensible offers. Finally, after some protracted negotiations, a deal was struck with a Camerounian company and the ship was sold on 14th August 2002 to Queen Makoua Charlotte of Douala.

What of the future? Well, Derick was back at sea, even before the *Candourity* had sailed from Guernsey. He is now in command in Allied Coasters Ltd., more or less where he began. He will probably remain at sea until he retires but it is doubtful if he will want to repeat the experience of being a shipowner. Unfortunately, it seems that the days of the small ship owner/master are passing if they have not already gone. Many masters have dreamed about owning their own ship but few have taken the plunge and, whatever regrets he might have, Derick actually did it and for better or worse, lived the dream for seventeen years.

Lancresse (2). *[Derick Goubert collection]*

Fleet list

1. MARY COAST 1985-1990.

ON 710009 399g 229n 515d 48.49 x 8.01 x 3.05 metres.

4-cyl. 4SCSA oil engine by N.V. Appingedammer Bronsmotorenfabriek, Appingedam, Netherlands.

1961: Completed by N.V. Scheepswerf 'Appingedam', Appingedam, Netherlands (Yard No. 189) for E. Wagenborg's Scheepvaart en Expeditiebedrijf N.V., Delfzijl, Netherlands as VECHTBORG.

1972: Sold to D.P. Geuze Bedrijf N.V. (E.Wagenborg's Scheepvaart en Expeditiebedrijf N.V.), Delfzijl, Netherlands and renamed ESPERANCE.

1973: Sold to K.B. Bos (E. Wagenborg's Scheepvaart en Expeditie-bedrijf N.V.), Delfzijl, Netherlands and renamed NOORDSTER.

1984: Sold to Harris and Dixon (Shipbrokers) Ltd., London (R. Lapthorn and Co. Ltd., Hoo, managers).

1985: Renamed MARY COAST and registered in Guernsey.

1986: Acquired by D.J. Goubert Shipping Ltd., Vale, Guernsey.

1990: Sold to Naviera Compasion de l'Eternal S. de R.C., Delray Beach, Florida, U.S.A. and renamed COMPASION DE L'ETERNAL. Registered at San Lorenzo, Honduras.

1991: Sold to Argo Maritime Co. S.A., Belize City, Belize and renamed KEY BISCAYNE.

1993: Sold to Alavar Marine Corporation, Belize City, Belize and renamed SPLASH.

1995: Renamed KEY BISCAYNE.

1995: Sold to Inversiones Richell Inc., San Pedro Sula, Honduras and renamed RICHELL VALERIA. Tonnages (ITC'69) became 386g 254n 515d.

Still in service 2003.

2. PORT SOIF 1990-1994.

ON 342979 429g 262n 645d 47.76 x 8.82 x 3.12 metres.

8-cyl. 4SCSA oil engine by English Electric Diesels Ltd., Kelvin Marine Division, Glasgow.

12.1971: Completed by N.V. Scheepswerf Gebr. Coops, Hoogezand, Netherlands (Yard No. 257) for Mardorf Peach and Co. Ltd., London as CATRINA WESTON.

1984: Sold to Custodian Leasing Ltd., Croydon (Whitbury Shipping Co. Ltd., Sheerness, managers) and renamed DELCE.

1987: Owner became Clientcare Ltd., Croydon.

5.4.1990: Acquired by D.J. Goubert Shipping Ltd., Vale, Guernsey (Marine Services Ltd., St. Peter Port, Guernsey, managers) and renamed PORT SOIF.

1991: Following breakdown, re-engined with an 8-cyl. 4SCSA oil engine made by G.E.C. Diesels Ltd. (Kelvin Marine Division), Glasgow.

21.12.1993: Struck Amfroque Rock off Herm while on passage from Alderney to St. Peter Port. Proceeded to St. Peter Port to discharge, thence to St. Sampsons for slipping. Subsequently declared a constructive total loss.

1994: Sold to S. Lyon-Smith, Teignmouth. Towed to Plymouth and later to Ramsgate for repairs.

1994: Sold to Bahamas Provider Line Ltd., Belize City, Belize and renamed BAHAMAS PROVIDER. Tonnages (ITC'69) became 436g 248n 645d.

Still in service 2003.

The first purchase, *Mary Coast* alongside at Goole. *[Charles Hill]*

Port Soif. [Derick Goubert]

Candourity. [Derick Goubert collection]

3. CANDOURITY 1992-2002
ON 365982 499g 330n 880d
56.11 x 9.89 x 3.25 metres.
6-cyl. 4SCSA oil engine by
Mirrlees Blackstone Ltd.,
Stamford.
11.1975: Completed by
Scheepswerf Bijlholt B.V.,
Foxhol, Netherlands (Yard No.
599) for F.T. Everard and Sons
Ltd., London as
CANDOURITY.
18.11.1992: Acquired by D.J.
Goubert Shipping Ltd., Vale,
Guernsey. Tonnages, (ITC'69)
became 559g 301n 880d.
14.8.2002: Sold to Queen
Makoua Charlotte, Douala,
Cameroun.
Still in service 2003.

4. LANCRESSE (1) 1994-1996.
ON 366445 664g 393n 953d
57.51 x 10.09 x 3.37 metres.
6-cyl. 4SCSA oil engine by
Mirrlees Blackstone Ltd.,
Stamford.
10.1978: Completed by
Jadewerft (Wilhelmshaven)

Lancresse (1). *[Derick Goubert]*

G.m.b.H., Wilhelmshaven, Germany
(Yard No. 144) for Shamrock Shipping
Co. Ltd., Larne (F.T. Everard and Sons
Management Ltd., London, managers) as
EDGAR DORMAN.
10.1981: Company and ship sold to
James Fisher and Sons PLC, Barrow-in-
Furness (F.T. Everard and Sons
Management Ltd., London, managers).
3.1984: Managers became J. and A.
Gardner and Co. (Management) Ltd.,
Glasgow.
9.1988: Owner became James Fisher and
Sons PLC, Barrow-in-Furness and
bareboat chartered to Dennison Shipping
Ltd., Kirkwall.
2.1989: Renamed BRESSAY SOUND.
3.1994: Repossessed by the owner on the
collapse of Dennison Shipping Ltd. and
laid up in Birkenhead.

4.1994: Acquired by D.J. Goubert
Shipping Ltd., Vale, Guernsey.
6.1994: Renamed LANCRESSE.
Tonnages (ITC'69) became 674g 366n
953d.
4.1996: Sold to Unicorn Ltd. (Alderney
Shipping Co. Ltd., managers), Guernsey.
10.1997: Renamed BURHOU I.
2001: Managers became Allied Coasters
Ltd., Guernsey.
Still in service 2003.

5. LANCRESSE (2) 1997-1999.
ON 900685 534g 241n 716d 49.71
x 8.34 x 3.47 metres.
6-cyl. 2SCSA oil engine by Alpha-
Diesel A/S., Frederikshavn, Denmark.
1975: Completed by A/S Nordsovaerftet,
Ringkoping, Denmark (Yard No. 99) for
Leo Abel Partrederi, Frederikshavn,

Denmark as PLATESSA. Original
tonnages were 300g 162n 716d.
1991: Sold to Partrederiet Fladstrand
(Nic Pedersen and Co.,
s'Maglerforretning, managers)
Frederikshavn, Denmark and renamed
TROJBERG. Gross tonnage became
299g.
1995: Sold to I/S Jenstar (H.C. Grube
I/S, manager) Marstal, Denmark and
renamed JENSTAR. Tonnages (ITC'69)
became 534g 241n 716d
10.1997: Acquired by D.J. Goubert
Shipping Ltd., Vale, Guernsey and
renamed LANCRESSE.
2.1999: Sold to Heri Thomsen A/S,
Gotu, Faroe Islands and renamed
SKURIN.
2000: Owner restyled Sp/f Heri
Thomsen.

Lancresse (2). *[Derick Goubert collection]*

PHOTOGRAPHER IN FOCUS: CLIFF PARSONS

Craig J.M. Carter

Many ship photographers have made their mark over the years in recording maritime history, but among the foremost in more recent times was Cliff Parsons, best remembered as the custodian of the merchant ship negative bank of the World Ship Photo Library for 25 years.

Born at Manchester, Cliff's home was in the Crumpsall district of the city. After wartime service in the Royal Navy, he became one of the earliest members of the Ship News Club, which later was to expand into the World Ship Society. Always out and about with his camera, he took many photographs of shipping in the Mersey and Manchester Ship Canal area, as well as in more distant ports. I can recall many a walk through the Liverpool docks with him, when his dry sense of humour added to the pleasure of watching and photographing ships.

His experience as librarian at the 'Daily Dispatch' newspaper and later at the 'News Chronicle' led to his involvement in the founding of the World Ship Photo Library and his huge collection of negatives, taken from the 1940s onwards, formed an invaluable part of the merchant ship section. He became custodian of that particular section of the Library, and his meticulous record keeping and the service he provided to members of the Society was incomparable. He also handled requests from museums, publishers and other individuals throughout the world for photographs, a further tribute to his dedication.

An enquiry to Cliff for photographs of a particular ship or ships was no problem. He would search through his files on his computer and would come up with a detailed list of what was available, describing the type of view - three-quarter bow, stern or whatever. Nothing was too much trouble for him.

Cliff remained a bachelor all his life, and after his retirement he devoted his time to his photography and his work with the Photo Library. A kind, unassuming gentleman, sadly he died on 28th June 1997, after a short illness.

The fact that the World Ship Society's negative collection has developed to the high level of importance that it now holds is a lasting tribute to Cliff. It stands as a living memorial to him.

The editors would like to thank David Whiteside, who took over as custodian of the World Ship Photo Library merchant ship negative collection from Cliff Parsons, for his considerable help in compiling this feature.

HELLENIC CHRYSSOULA
(opposite)
*John Crown and Sons Ltd.,
Sunderland; 1910, 1,441gt, 240 feet
T. 3-cyl. by Richardsons, Westgarth
and Co. Ltd., Sunderland.*
Cliff has left some excellent portrayals
of the Manchester Ship Canal and
Mersey. Here *Hellenic Chryssoula*
loads coal or coke at Partington in
April 1949. The Panamanian-
registered ship had been built as a
collier, the *Bondicar* of Broomhill
Collieries Ltd., Newcastle-upon-Tyne.
In 1946 she was sold to a London-
Greek, E.P. Yannoulatos who first
renamed her *Chryssoula*, adding the
Hellenic prefix in 1947. *Hellenic
Chryssoula* arrived at Newport to be
broken up by John Cashmore Ltd. in
June 1954.

MERSEY NO. 4 (above)
*Fleming and Ferguson Ltd., Paisley;
1945, 683gt, 168 feet
Two T. 3-cyl. by Fleming and Ferguson
Ltd., Paisley; twin screws.*
One of the Mersey Docks and Harbour
Board craft which maintained the
necessary depth of water in the Mersey
and its approaches, the prosaically-
named hopper *Mersey No. 4* is seen
against the background of Clarence
Dock Power Station in July 1954.
Built as the *Empire
Heathland*, she ran as *Mersey No. 4*
from 1947 to 1964, subsequently
becoming *WD Beta* and *WK Beta*.

CITADEL (below)
*Scheepswerf 'De Waal' N.V.,
Zaltbommel; 1950, 369gt, 138 feet
4-cyl. 4SCSA oil engine by
Maschinenfabriek Augsburg-Nurnberg
A.G., Augsburg.*
Heading into the Mersey in May 1951
is the Dutch coaster *Citadel*, owned by
R.Huizenga of Groningen, and part of
the huge fleet managed by N.V.
'Carebeka'. She passed to UK owners
towards the end of her career, being
owned from 1971 by various
companies and individuals in East
Anglia or London. A fire which gutted
her accommodation in 1974
effectively meant the end of her career,
and after a long lay up *Citadel* was
broken up Belgium in 1978.

CADISHEAD (above)

J. Cran and Somerville Ltd., Leith; 1917, 154gt, 85 feet

C. 2-cyl. by J. Cran and Somerville Ltd., Leith.

Cliff has left us some excellent portraits of Manchester Ship Canal tugs. In May 1949 *Cadishead* is shown at Runcorn. Note the interesting variety of craft in the Tidal Dock in the background, including a small steamer, a small tug, the rail-mounted steam cranes, and the material piled on the quayside. The name Flint Wharf gives a clue to the nature of this material.

Built as *H.S. 31* for the Government during the First World War, *Cadishead* was acquired from W.J. Reynolds of Plymouth in 1926. The steamer remained on the Ship Canal's strength until 1960 when she was broken up.

MOUNT MANISTY (below)

J. Cran and Somerville Ltd., Leith; 1917, 154gt, 85 feet

C. 2-cyl. by J. Cran and Somerville Ltd., Leith.

The portrait of *Mount Manisty* as head tug on a Ship Canal tow in September 1956 was almost certainly taken to commemorate the appointment as her skipper of Jim Nelson, whom Cliff would know through the World Ship Society in Manchester. Although not clear in the print, the fender on the bow carries an 'L' plate put there by her crew to remind Jim he had much to learn! Like Cliff, Jim also came to play an important role in the World Ship Society, and was known to many members as Mutual Interests Secretary.

Mount Manisty was a sister of *Cadishead*, and their careers ran in parallel. She was built as *H.S.31*, on sale by the Government ran for W.J. Reynolds until 1926, and survived as *Mount Manisty* until broken up in 1961.

THISTLEMUIR (above)
J.L. Thompson and Sons Ltd., Sunderland; 1942, 7,237gt, 441 feet
T. 3-cyl. by the North Eastern Marine Engineering Co. (1938) Ltd., Sunderland.

The *Thistlemuir* of 1942 appears very much a wartime standard ship, but was in fact built for the account of her owners, the Albyn Line Ltd., rather than the Government as an 'Empire' ship. The resemblance is not surprising, as her builders were the instigators of the design adopted not just for British war-built ships, but also for many built in North America.

Seen here in July 1955, the *Thistlemuir* steamed on until 1961 when Spanish owners put her under the Panama flag as *Nunez de Balboa*, as which she was broken up at Osaka in 1968. By then her original owners had gone, liquidated in 1966, and with them the last appearance of Sunderland on the stern of an ocean-going ship.

EMPIRE ELY (below)
Lübecker Flenderwerke A.G., Lübeck; 1948, 6,113gt, 455 feet
C. 4-cyl. with low pressure turbine by Danzigerwerft, Danzig.

In April 1951, *Empire Ely* is discharging at the flour mills at Birkenhead, in full Ropner's colours with their distinctive green hull. But she was hardly a typical Ropner tramp.

At the end of the war she was captured incomplete at Lübeck, where she was being built for Norddeutscher Lloyd as the cargo liner *Greifswald*. She was completed for the Ministry of Transport, who placed her under Ropner's management. Themselves operating a cargo liner service to the US Gulf, Ropners thought about buying her and even allocated the name *Swiftpool* to her, but evidently thought better of it. After several changes of managers she was sold to the Chandris group as *Maribella*. In 1955 she went back to Germany, as Detjen's *Ganges*, following which was a further spell with Greek owners as *Eleni* before she was broken up at Santander in 1972.

VERONICA TENNANT (above)
Mistley Shipbuilding and Repairing Co., Mistley; 1927, 397gt, 142 feet
C. 2-cyl. by Crabtree and Co.Ltd., Great Yarmouth.

At Fowey in August 1951, the crew of *Veronica Tennant* hang some of their washing out, presumably after loading a cargo of china clay for a port in the north west.

At least three builders had a hand in the completion of this steam coaster. She had been laid down by Colby Brothers Ltd., Lowestoft as their yard number 21 but had not been completed when the yard closed. The Great Yarmouth builder Pitchers Ltd. launched her in March 1922, but she was then taken to Mistley for fitting out. The name of her official builders, Mistley Shipbuilding and Repairing Co., hid local barge and coaster owners of the Horlock family, who ran her as *Ipswich Trader* until 1946.

Her second career began in 1946 when sold to Duff, Herbert and Mitchell Ltd. of Liverpool and renamed *Veronica Tennant*. The owners were connected with Dinorwic Slate Quarries Ltd. in North Wales, and the ship actually passed to quarry ownership in 1953: but already in 1951 the quarries initials were painted on her funnel. However, she carried little if any slate, as in any case the quarry's production was by now fast declining, but tramped around the west coast. Her arrival at Llanelly in November 1954 to be broken up by Rees Shipbreaking Industries Ltd. brought an end to the career of a fascinating little ship.

BALLYDOUGAN (below)
Scott and Sons, Bowling; 1913, 579gt, 179 feet
T. 3-cyl. by Aitchison, Blair and Co. Ltd., Glasgow.

Like many steam coasters still running in the 1950s, *Ballydougan* was something of a veteran, having been completed for John Kelly Ltd., Belfast over 43 years before this photograph was taken in June 1956. She was originally *Carnalea*, but was renamed in 1952 after acquisition of her owners by Stephenson, Clarke decreed that all Kelly's colliers should have 'Bally' names. She steamed on until 1959, when sold to breakers in Pembroke Dock who sold her on to Belgian shipbreakers.

DUCHESS OF FIFE (opposite top)
Fairfield Shipbuilding and Engineering Co. Ltd., Govan; 1903, 336gt, 210 feet
T. 4-cyl. by Barclay, Curle and Co. Ltd., Glasgow.

It's June 1952 on the Clyde, and *Duchess of Fife*'s entire complement of passengers wear their rain coats. Not a single passenger is on the lower deck: is this thanks to Scottish hardiness, or some regulation that did not allow them down there until the bar opened?

This was last full year of service for one of the fastest and most popular paddle steamers on the Clyde. The Caledonian Steam Packet Co. Ltd. laid up *Duchess of Fife* in June 1953, and that September disposed of her for scrap to Smith and Houston Ltd.

CHINDIT (below)
J. Hay and Sons Ltd., Kirkintilloch;
1945, 74gt, 61 feet
C. 2-cyl.
Another delightful Scottish view from June 1952, but the location is unidentified. Hay's puffer *Chindit* is sailing from a small harbour on the Clyde, probably after discharging a cargo of domestic coal, and her small crew will be thinking of going below for a rest.

    Chindit was the last vessel built at Hays' Kirkintilloch yard, being launched on 20th September 1945, and taken to Port Dundas to have her engine fitted. In 1960 she broke away from her moorings at Dunoon Pier and bumped along the shore, severely damaging herself. She was brought back to be slipped and examined at Hay's yard at Kirkintilloch, but was found to be not worth repairing, and was demolished at Bowling.

SAMARIA (above)
*Cammell, Laird and Co. Ltd.,
Birkenhead; 1921, 19,848gt, 602 feet
Six steam turbines geared to two shafts
by Cammell, Laird and Co. Ltd.,
Birkenhead.*

Cliff's negatives usually carry the date
they were taken, and the August 1952
date identifies this shot of *Samaria* as
being taken at Southampton, the
Cunarder having been put on the
service from there to Quebec in 1951.
Originally she had run out of Liverpool
to Halifax and Boston. *Samaria* was
one of three sisters, part of a bigger
group of basically similar passenger
ships built for Cunard just after the
First World War. Despite her age,
Samaria was to represent Cunard at
the Coronation Review at Spithead in
June 1953. She was broken up at
Inverkeithing early in 1956.

UNITED STATES (below)
*Newport News Shipbuilding and
Drydock Company, Newport News,
Virginia; 1952, 53,329gt, 917 feet
Four steam turbines driving quadruple
screws by the Westinghouse Electrical
and Manufacturing Co., Easington,
Pennsylvania.*

Probably on the same visit as he
photographed *Samaria,* Cliff caught
the *United States,* which had entered
service only in July, winning the Blue
Riband on her maiden voyage. With
her huge funnels - which for once
reflected the enormous power of her
engines - she made a fascinating
contrast with the rather staid design of
the Cunarders then using
Southampton. Sawyer and Mitchell in
'From America to United States' note
that the funnels were of uneven size,
with the forward one being higher, and
that the bands on the funnels were of
markedly different widths, all to
preserve visual symmetry.

Few other commercial ships
can have kept so many secrets in
peacetime as the *United States*: it was
not until 1968 that her 42-knot speed
and 240,000 horse power were
declassified. Even her underwater lines
were regarded as confidential, and a
full-hull model of the ship on display in
New York had its underwater hull
hidden in a plaster 'sea'.

As these notes are written, 51
years after the *United States'* maiden
voyage, there are once again plans to
put the ship back in service. There
must be doubts that such an ambitious
scheme could be funded, but there are
many who would love to see again the
sight depicted in Cliff's photograph.

BRAEMAR CASTLE (above)
Harland and Wolff Ltd., Belfast; 1952, 17,029gt, 556 feet
Parsons' double-reduction steam turbines by Harland and Wolff Ltd., Belfast.
Trips to Southampton in August must have been a feature of Cliff's life in the 1950s, as this is August 1953 and the subject is *Braemar Castle.* She was intended by Union-Castle to be an intermediate ship, initially for the round Africa service, but she deputised for the faster Southampton to Capetown mail ships on a number of occasions during her career. Sadly,

this was to be rather short, and when only 13 years old, she was laid at London in 1965, and broken up at Faslane early the next year.

PORT VINDEX (below)
Swan, Hunter and Wigham Richardson Ltd., Wallsend-on-Tyne; 1944, 10,489gt, 524 feet
Two oil engines 5-cyl. 2SCSA by Swan, Hunter and Wigham Richardson Ltd., Wallsend-on-Tyne.
Photographed in June 1954, the name of *Port Vindex* was a reminder of her wartime role. Her hull, building at Wallsend, was taken over by the

Admiralty in 1943 and was completed as an aircraft carrier, HMS *Vindex.* Only four escort carriers were completed in British yards, as the USA was mass producing them, and lent no fewer than 39 to the Royal Navy. HMS *Vindex* was re-acquired by Port Line after the war, along with HMS *Nairana* which became *Port Victor.* Rebuilt by Swan, Hunter as a conventional cargo ship, *Port Vindex* entered service in June 1949 and then led a relatively peaceful life until arriving at Kaohsiung for demolition in August 1971.

THE IRON LADIES Part 3
John Harrison

Conversions

Like the redundant church or cinema, the redundant ore carrier presents the problem of a purpose-built structure no longer required for the function for which it was designed. By the end of the charter periods, the average size of ore carriers had significantly increased and in a number of cases their owners decided that the ships should be converted to other uses. Although no longer considered suitable for ore carrier use, these ships had strong hulls capable of many more years' service and with engines aft they offered more versatile units than conventional cargo vessels with engines amidships. The Port Talbot type has proved particularly popular for conversion, no doubt a reflection of their small size making them particularly unviable as ore carriers.

Several of the ships were converted for oil exploration work. The first of these ships to be so converted was the *Oregis*. She arrived at Swan Hunter's repair yard in April 1973 for conversion to a diving support and oil well maintenance vessel. A number of alterations were carried out. Her third hold was converted to a moonpool with an additional deck being added inside the main deck to enable equipment to be handled in a sheltered environment. A smaller diving moonpool was also fitted. Six 10-ton mooring anchors were added, handled by 75-ton pull winches. Other facilities included a helideck mounted on the bows, a 17$\frac{1}{2}$-ton crane, a diving gantry, decompression chambers and additional accommodation in Portacabins. Her engines were unaltered, though two additional generators were fitted in her engine room.

Originally it was intended that the *Oregis* would be fitted out in France prior to being used to weld an underwater pipeline in the Mediterranean on charter to Hydro-Tech Services during spring 1974. On 10th March 1974 she was leaving the Tyne en route to France on her first voyage following conversion when her engines failed and she ran aground on the Black Midden Rocks at the entrance to the Tyne. One of her assisting tugs, the *Northsider* (156/1957) owned by Lawson-Batey Tugs Ltd., in a vain attempt to prevent the *Oregis* running aground, also grounded. The *Oregis* stranded in a position such that her fore end was left unsupported at low tide. Her hull started to buckle abreast her moonpool as this was its weakest point. To prevent her breaking in two temporary strengthening had to be fitted to her hull at this point.

The *Oregis* was not refloated until 8th April, the *Northsider* having been refloated on 25th March. The *Oregis*' hull had been badly hogged as a result of her grounding. To correct this a cut was made from the keel of the ship to almost the main deck through a section and the ship's own weight was used to pull the hull back to its correct position. This work was carried out at Swan Hunter's repair yard where she remained till 6th September. To minimise delay in bringing the ship into service during this time, fitting out which was originally to have been carried out in France was undertaken.

Her initial charter to Hydro-Tech Services, in anticipation of which she had been named *H.T.S. Coupler 1*, fell through as a result of the grounding. Nevertheless, the conversion of the *Oregis* proved to be a successful and lucrative one. The cost of her conversion was repaid comparatively quickly. In September 1979, however, her 25-year surveys became due and she was laid up on the Tyne. Because of rust working through her hull she was in need of major repairs and Houlders were reluctant to have this work carried out without a further charter available. The return from such a charter would have made the work viable. Apart from a short period working in the Humber where she was taken under tow, she remained on the Tyne until she was sold to Spanish shipbreakers in November 1982. At one point Houlders considered fitting her with a second-hand dynamic positioning system taken from the semi-submersible diving support vessel *Seaway Swan*, owned by Seaway Offshore Work Platform A/S, when she was converted to a drilling rig in 1981. This project did not go ahead, however, and when Houlders built a replacement diving support vessel she was sold for scrap. Interestingly the name chosen for the replacement ship was *Orelia*, the name of the first of the ships in the *Oregis*' class. The reason for this choice of names was apparently that Houlders considered both ships to be ahead of their time in terms of design.

Another Port Talbot type ship to be converted for oil exploration was Salvesen Offshore Holdings Ltd.'s *Gullane*, the former *Philippe L.D.* She arrived at the North East Coast Ship Repairers' Middle Yard, South Shields, in November 1974 for conversion to a drillship. All her accommodation was removed and rebuilt, fully air-conditioned, with additional accommodation for construction and other workers being provided. A new helideck was fitted, as were eight primary and eight secondary anchors. To make the ship more stable, sponsons were fitted to the side of her hull. Two 100-ton cranes were provided. A 'pipe rack' or additional deck for handling drill pipe was fitted above the main deck. Underwater facilities included a television camera with three 1,000-watt lights capable of working 1,000 feet below sea level. The main feature of her conversion, however, was the addition of a 162 feet (50 metre) high drilling rig in the centre of the ship, capable of drilling to 20,000 feet (6,000 metres) in 1,000 feet (300 metres) of water. Her engines were removed and replaced by four 2,200 bhp diesel-electric units, each connected to a 1,500 kW alternator supplying power to four 1,000 hp electric motors, geared to a single screw shaft. Diesel-electric machinery is common in ships for this type of work. The project cost $31,000,000 and was at that time the largest conversion job carried out in a British ship repair yard. At the end of her conversion she was renamed *Dalkeith*. Unfortunately a projected charter in South America fell through and she was laid up on the Tyne for some time before being chartered to City Drilling Services Ltd. for whom she was renamed *Wingate*.

Houlders acquired another Port Talbot type ship with a view to converting to a flexible pipe layer as a companion to the *Oregis*. This was the *Ravensworth* which they acquired from Dalgliesh 1975. This project did not go ahead, however, and within a few months she was resold to Flexservice N.V., part of the Ugland group, who themselves converted her to a flexible pipe layer under the name *Flexservice 1*. She arrived at the yard of Kristiansands Mekaniska Verksted A/S in November 1975 for this conversion. The work was carried out in two stages and between these two stages she was employed in the

North Sea. Thus, her conversion was not completed till the summer of 1977. The work involved the repositioning of watertight bulkheads to enable the holds to take the drums or 'baskets' of flexible pipe. A basket for flexible pipe was fitted to the main deck. To accommodate this plus winches and deckhouses, all hatch covers had to be removed. A helideck was fitted at the stern and side sponsons were added for greater stability. Handling gear for launching and laying out piping, including a 25-ton crane, was fitted at the bow. This equipment could unload four different diameter pipelines at the same time. She was fitted with a computer-controlled dynamic positioning system. This

worked off four 1,160 hp retractable Schottel units, two at the bow and two at the stern, and a 700 hp stern thruster. Two additional auxiliary engine rooms had to be provided fore and aft to house the machinery for the Schottel units.

Two other ships have been converted for oil exploration, both to drillships. In 1975 the Port Talbot type, *Zapata Trader,* ex *Naess Trader*, was converted to a drillship and fitted with diesel electric machinery at Jacksonville, Florida. On 23rd September 1981, the *Australind,* originally the Newport type vessel, *Queensgarth,* arrived at Keppel Shipyard for conversion to a drillship.

Above: *Flexservice 1,* the plan below showing features incorporated.

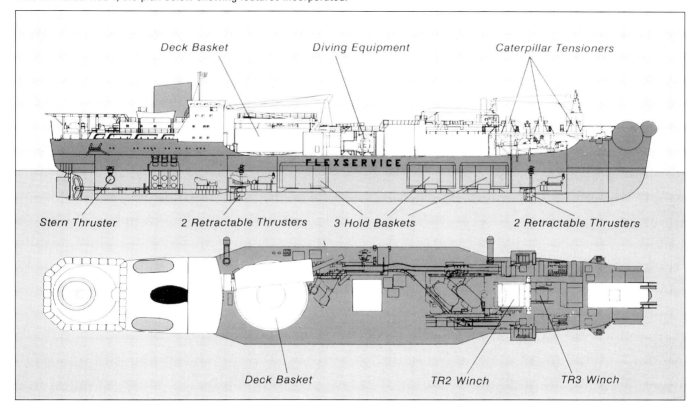

Other uses

A bar and shallow waters at the mouth of the River Plate prevent the largest bulk carriers entering the river loaded. Thus there is a need for a vessel to act as a lightening ship and the *Astrapatricia* was converted for this purpose. She was originally the *Welsh Herald*, one of the largest type of ore carriers. The conversion took place at Hapag Lloyd's Yard, Bremerhaven between November 1976 and February 1977. Following the completion of this work, the ship was used to lighten cargoes of ore and coal entering the River Plate and also for 'topping up' outward-bound cargoes of grain. Alterations carried out included the installation of a 1,000 hp bow thruster, three cranes with ore and coal grabs and three conveyor belts, plus alterations to her accommodation. At the same time the main engine was given a complete overhaul and repairs were carried out to her cargo section.

Two other ships have been converted for other uses, the *LSCO Tawi-Tawi*, originally the Port Talbot type *Crinan*, was converted to an ore-oil carrier in 1977 and in 1983 under the name of *Lake Taal* she was again converted, this time to a bulk carrier.

At the end of her charter period in 1969, another Port Talbot type, the *Essex*, was converted to a bulk chemical tanker, the *Essi Anne*, for carrying lead additive for petrol made by Octel at Ellesmere Port. It should be noted that this conversion had obviously not entailed the use of all her holds as, when she was broken up, she took on her final voyage from Cardiff to Gadani Beach a cargo of scrap iron. Hatch covers that had been welded shut were re-opened for this purpose. For this final voyage she was renamed *E. Anne* and, according to her stern registered in 'Valetta'. The scrapping of the *Essi Anne* is in contrast to the fate of a 'sister ship' (in the looser meaning of the term) used for the same purpose, the *Essi Kari* (10,696/1956) which was scuttled in deep water in the Atlantic on 26th April 1982 because demolition was considered too dangerous as a result of the cargo she had carried.

Although perhaps better described as an adaptation rather than a conversion, mention should be made to the work that was carried out to the four St. Denis Shipping Co. Ltd.'s vessels, *Dukesgarth*, *Knightsgarth*, *Monksgarth* and *Queensgarth* in the early 1970s. These were adapted for the carriage of grain by fitting grain scuttles to each wing ballast tank. Two vessels were converted by Cammell, Lairds, Birkenhead and two by Swan Hunters, Wallsend. This had to be done to fulfil sub-charter to Federal Commerce of Canada for whom grain was to be carried in addition to steel and steel products. The charter arrangements fell through, however, and only a few voyages were made.

In addition to these conversions, three ships were converted for non-seagoing uses. The *Ripon* was sold to Spanish shipbreakers, but resold to Latasa S.A., Spain and converted for use as a hulk for lightening coal-carrying bulk carriers at Santurce, Spain, having been fitted with a Munck loader. The *Halkis Express*, formerly the largest type vessel, *Victore,* was permanently moored at Chalkis, Greece for use as a cement storage vessel. Similarly the *Alfa Cementa*, formerly the Newport type *Dunadd*, was reported as being used as a cement silo and storage facility in Saudi Arabia in 1978 and was deleted from 'Lloyd's Register' in 1980.

Conclusion

This interesting chapter in the history of shipping ended on 14th February 2001 when the *Service*, ex-*Flexservice 1*, originally the *Ravensworth*, arrived at the breaker's yard in Alang. I would like to think that somebody on board recognised the significance of the occasion, but I suspect all they thought was that another old ship was reaching an inevitable end.

The chemical tanker *Essi Anne,* formerly the *Essex*, arriving at Eastham in June 1973. [*J. and M. Clarkson*]

FLEET LIST (part three)

MAVROLEON BROTHERS (SHIP MANAGEMENT) LTD.
Falaise Ore Carriers Ltd. (Mavroleon Brothers (Ship Management) Ltd.), London

FINNAMORE MEADOW 1961-1977
O.N. 302845 13,057g 7,432n 18,420d
534'7" x 70'5" x 29'8¾"
4-cyl. 2SCSA Doxford-type oil engine by North Eastern Marine Engineering Co. Ltd., Wallsend-on-Tyne; 670 x 2,320, 4,500 BHP, 12 knots.
6.9.1961: Launched by Austin and Pickersgill Ltd., Sunderland (Yard No. 378) for Falaise Ore Carriers Ltd. (Mavroleon Brothers (Ship Management) Ltd., managers), London as FINNAMORE MEADOW.
9.1961: Completed.
1977: Owners became Seas Carriers Corporation, Monrovia, Liberia (Mavroleon Brothers Ltd., London) and renamed DON MANUEL under the Greek flag.
1981: Sold to Palamadis Shipping Ltd., Monrovia, Liberia (Armada Marine SA (A.S. Manes), Piraeus, Greece) and renamed PALAMIDI under the Greek flag.
1.4.1982: Arrived at Vigo for demolition by Miguel Martins Pereira.
24.5.1982: Work commenced.

Traditional Traders Ltd. (Mavroleon Brothers (Ship Management) Ltd.), London

VICTORE (L) 1963-1978
O.N. 305884 19,543g 9,852n 28,342d
615'0" x 84'6" x 32'0¼"
6-cyl. 2SCSA Gotaverken-type oil engines by North Eastern Marine Engineering Co. Ltd., Wallsend-on-Tyne; 760 x 1500, 7,500 BHP, 13 knots.
19.8.1963: Launched by Austin and Pickersgill Ltd., Sunderland (Yard No. 831) for Traditional Traders Ltd. (Mavroleon Brothers (Ship Management) Ltd., managers), London as VICTORE.
12.1963: Completed.
1978: Sold to Halkis Cement Co. SA (N. Demetriades and M. Keusseoglou), Athens, Greece and renamed HALKIS EXPRESS.
1980: Owners became Finda Transport and Enterprises SA (N. Demetriades and M. Keusseoglou), Athens.
22.7.1980: Arrived at Chalkis for conversion to a cement storage vessel and subsequently permanently moored at Chalkis.

NAESS DENHOLM AND CO. LTD., GLASGOW
This company was jointly owned by Erling Naess (60%) and J. and J. Denholm Ltd. (40%).

Top to bottom: *Finnamore Meadow, Victore* (both docking at South Wales ports), *Naess Trader* at Eastham on 18th April 1971. *[J. and M. Clarkson]*

NAESS TRADER (PT) 1957-1973
O.N. 187263 6,853g 3,103n 9,290d
425'6" x 57'3" x 25'4"
3-cyl. 2SCSA Doxford-type oil engine by North Eastern Marine Engineering Co. Ltd., Wallsend-on-Tyne; 600 x 2,320, 2,600 BHP, 11¼ knots.
12.6.1957: Launched by William Pickersgill and Sons Ltd., Sunderland (Yard No. 354) for Naess Denholm and Co. Ltd., Glasgow as NAESS TRADER.
9.1957: Completed.
1973: Sold to Zapata North Sea Ltd., Panama (Zapata Corporation, Houston, Texas, USA) and renamed ZAPATA TRADER.
1975: Converted to drilling ship at Jacksonville. Gross tonnage now 6,516. Fitted with diesel electric machinery, three 6-cyl. 2SCSA oil engines, 230 x 254, 4,364 kW (5,850 BHP) driving three generators each 1,400 kW ac connected to two electric motors each of 1,492 kW (2,000 SHP) single-reduction geared to screw shaft by General Motors Corporation, USA.
1979: Sold to Perforaciones Maritimas Mexicanas SA, Nueva Leon, Mexico (Construcciones Protexa SA de CV, Mexico City, Mexico) and renamed CORA under the Panama flag.
1979: Owners became Petroleos Mexicanos, Mexico City.
1983: Sold to Zapata Marine Service Ltd. SA, Panama (Zapata Corporation, Houston, Texas, USA) and renamed ZAPATA TRADER.
1986: Owners became Zapata North Sea Inc., Panama.
17.6.1987: Demolition commenced by National Shipbreakers Pte. Ltd., Singapore.

SILVER LINE LTD.
Bishopsgate Shipping Co. Ltd., London

This company was a joint venture between BISC (Ore), Silver Line, Sir J. Laing and Sons and Thompsons.

ALDERSGATE 1960-1975

O.N. 301180 12,718g 5,677n 18,220d
525'0" x 70'3" x 29'6½"
4-cyl. 2SCSA Doxford-type oil engines by William Doxford and Sons (Engineering) Ltd., Sunderland; 670 x 2,320, 4,400 BHP, 12.5 knots.
26.2.1960: Launched by Sir James Laing and Sons Ltd., Sunderland (Yard No. 824) for Bishopsgate Shipping Ltd., London as ALDERSGATE.
7.1960: Completed.
14.9.1965: Collided with the tug YEWGARTH (274/1943 R. and J.H. Rea Ltd.) off Queen Alexandra Dock entrance, Cardiff. The YEWGARTH was damaged beyond repair.
1969: Renamed SILVERSHORE.
1975: Owners became Coralstone Shipping Corporation, Monrovia, Liberia (Navigation and Coal Trade Co. Ltd. (Boris Vlasov), London) and renamed PUERTO MADRYN.
1977: Sold to Danube Shipping Co. Ltd., Limassol, Cyprus (G. Georgopoulos Maritime Co. Ltd., Piraeus, Greece) and renamed DANUBE.
3.4.1984: Arrived at Chittagong for demolition by MEB Corporation having been sold to them through German interests.

BISHOPSGATE 1959-1975

O.N. 165486 12,785g, 6,750n 18,060d
535'10" x 70'3" x 29'6½"
4-cyl. 2SCSA Doxford-type oil engines by William Doxford and Sons (Engineering) Ltd., Sunderland; 670 x 2,320, 4,400 BHP, 12.5 knots.
30.11.1959: Launched by Sir James Laing and Sons Ltd., Sunderland (Yard No. 823) for Bishopsgate Shipping Ltd., London as BISHOPSGATE.
4.1960: Completed.
1969: Owners became St. Helens Shipping Co. Ltd., London and renamed BEECHWOOD.
1975: Sold to Nea Presdokia Maritime Co. SA (Comninos Brothers Shipping Co. SA, Piraeus, Greece) and renamed NICOLAS C.
1975: Sold to Pafos Shipping Co. SA, Piraeus, Greece.
1977: Sold to Fenecia di Navigazione S.p.A, Cagliari (Landi & C., Genoa), Italy and renamed CAPITAN FRANCO. V.
10.11.1986: Arrived Porto Nogaro for demolition by Acciaiere di Porto Nogaro.
1.1987: Demolition commenced.

Top to bottom: *Aldersgate, Silvershore, Bishopsgate, Beechwood.* [J. and M. Clarkson]

28

Above: *Silvercrag* in May 1960. Below: *Silversand* sailing from Swansea. *[J. and M. Clarkson]*

St. Helens Shipping Co. Ltd., London

SILVERCRAG 1958-1973
O.N. 300798 10,885g 5,725n 15,465d
503'5" x 70'0" x 28'0¾"
4-cyl. 2SCSA Doxford-type oil engine by William Doxford and Sons (Engineering) Ltd., Sunderland; 670 x 2,320, 4,400 BHP, 12.75 knots.
18.7.1958: Launched by Sir James Laing and Sons Ltd., Sunderland (Yard No. 816) for St. Helens Shipping Co. Ltd., London as SILVERCRAG.
12.1958: Completed.
1969: Renamed CHERRYWOOD.
1973: Sold to Eskikdale Shipping Co. SA, Panama (Seven Seas Maritime Ltd. (B.S. Kalamotusis and P.E. Kollakis), London) and renamed

KAPPA VICTORY under the Greek flag.
1980: Renamed RIO VICTORY.
1980: Sold to Astromar Shipping Inc., Monrovia, Liberia (Mec Marine Consultants Ltd., London) and renamed ANNABELLE E under the Greek flag.
19.9.1982: Arrived at Gadani Beach for demolition by Haji Abdullah Kassim and Co.

SILVERSAND 1958-1973
O.N. 187769 10,887g 5,725n 15,465d
503'5" x 70'0" x 28'0¾"
4-cyl. 2SCSA Doxford-type oil engines by William Doxford and Sons (Engineering) Ltd., Sunderland;670 x 2,320, 4,400 BHP, 12.5 knots.
21.1.1958: Launched by Sir James

Laing and Sons Ltd., Sunderland (Yard No. 814) for St. Helens Shipping Co. Ltd., London as SILVERSAND.
5.1958: Completed.
1969: Owners became Bishopsgate Shipping Co. Ltd., London.
1973: Sold to Compania Alecos SA, Panama (Companhia Dapo SA (N.A. Davaris), Piraeus, Greece) for £200,000 and renamed ALECOS under the Greek flag.
14.9.1975: Struck wreck and ran aground off Los Cobezos, five miles west of Tarifa in position 36.05.57 north by 05.43.08 west during a voyage from Melilla to Sczecin with iron ore pellets.
15.9.1975: Abandoned by her crew and subsequently broke in two.

W.A. SOUTER AND CO. LTD.
Bamburgh Shipping Co. Ltd. (WA Souter and Co. Ltd., managers), Newcastle-upon-Tyne
Bamburgh Shipping Co. Ltd. was jointly owned by W.A. Souter and Co. Ltd. and BISC Ore Ltd.

BAMBURGH CASTLE 1969-1975
O.N. 186891 11,894g, 6,252n 17,075d
512'2" x 70'3" x 29'6"
4-cyl. 2SCSA Doxford-type oil engine by Swan Hunter and Wigham Richardson Ltd., Newcastle-upon-Tyne; 670 x 2,320, 4,200 BHP, 12 knots.
24.2.1959: Launched by Swan Hunter and Wigham Richardson Ltd., Newcastle-upon-Tyne (Yard No. 1950) for Bamburgh Shipping Co. Ltd. (W.A. Souter and Co. Ltd., managers), Newcastle-upon-Tyne as BAMBURGH CASTLE.
6.1959: Completed.
1975: Sold to Toxotis Shipping Co. SA, Panama (E. Pothitos, E. Koutsofios and others, Piraeus, Greece) and renamed EVA.
21.5.1984: Left Yawata having been sold to Chinese shipbreakers and arrived at a Chinese port prior to 1 June 1984.

CHEVIOT 1960-1977
O.N. 186914 13,082g 6,017n 18,385d
525'0" x 70'3" x 29'9"
5-cyl. 2SCSA Sulzer-type oil engines by George Clark (Sunderland) Ltd., Sunderland; 720 x 1,250, 4,500 BHP, 12¼ knots.
19.12.1960: Launched by Austin and Pickersgill Ltd., Sunderland (Yard No. 367) for Bamburgh Shipping Co. Ltd. (W.A. Souter and Co. Ltd., managers), Newcastle-upon-Tyne as CHEVIOT.
3.1961: Completed.
1977: Sold to Compania Evpo SA, Panama (Dapo Shipping SA (N.A. Davaris), Piraeus, Greece) and renamed DAPO TRADER under the Greek flag.
1984: Sold to Trico Corporation SA, Panama (N.V. and T. Tricoglou, Piraeus, Greece) and renamed TRADER under the Greek flag.
About 1.7.1984: Arrived Setubal for demolition.
5.11.1984: Work commenced.
This ship never operated commercially under the name TRADER. She had been laid up at Galixidi under the name DAPO TRADER on 11.6.1982 and the only voyage she made under the name TRADER was from there to the breakers at Setubal.

LINDISFARNE 1960-1975
O.N. 186903 12,733g, 5,633n 18,280d
525'0" x 70'3" x 29'6½"
4-cyl. 2SCSA Doxford-type oil engine by William Doxford and Sons (Engineers) Ltd., Sunderland; 670 x 2,320, 4,400 BHP, 12 knots.
28.3.1960: Launched by Joseph L.

Top to bottom: *Bamburgh Castle* in March 1962, a rusty *Cheviot* in the Mersey on 7th June 1976, *Lindisfarne*. [J. and M. Clarkson]

Thompson and Sons Ltd., Sunderland (Yard No. 699) for Bamburgh Shipping Co. Ltd. (W.A. Souter and Co. Ltd., managers), Newcastle-upon-Tyne as LINDISFARNE.
7.1960: Completed.
1975: Sold to Singapore Cosmos Shipping Co. (Pte.) Ltd., Singapore and renamed COSMOS TRADERS.
1977: Owners became Inter-Globe Navigation Co. (Pte.) Ltd. (Singapore Cosmos Shipping Co. (Pte.) Ltd.), Singapore.
1979: Sold to the Korea Tonghae Shipping Co. (Government of the Democratic People's Republic of North Korea), Pyongyang, North Korea and renamed BONG SAN.
4.1996: Reported sold to Chinese shipbreakers.

LONGSTONE 1960-1975

O.N. 186908 13,062g 6,007n 18,320d 525'0" x 70'3" x 29'8"
5-cyl. 2SCSA Sulzer-type oil engines by George Clark (Sunderland) Ltd., Sunderland; 720 x 1,250, 4,500 BHP, 12 knots.
24.8.1960: Launched by Austin and Pickersgill Ltd., Sunderland (Yard No. 366) for Bamburgh Shipping Co. Ltd. (W.A. Souter and Co. Ltd., managers), Newcastle-upon-Tyne as LONGSTONE.
10.1960: Completed.
1975: Sold to Matat Shipping Co. SA, Panama (John D. Polemis, London) and renamed PARNASSOS.
1977: Transferred to Greek registry.
30.8.1982: Laid up at Eleusis.
1985: Sold to Amesa Shipping Ltd., Gibraltar (Anro Marine Enterprises SA, Piraeus, Greece) and renamed AMESA TRIA.
14.8.1985: Left Bombay having been sold to KS Steel for demolition.
13.10.1985: Demolition began at Sitalpur.

These ships were named after landmarks in the Bamburgh area of Northumberland. Longstone Lighthouse, Cheviot Hill and Lindisfarne Island are all visible from Bamburgh Castle.

Sheaf Steam Shipping Co. Ltd. (W.A. Souter and Co. Ltd., managers), Newcastle-upon-Tyne

SHEAF FIELD 1958-1969

O.N. 186888 10,882g, 5,713n 15,455d 503'5" x 70'0" x 28'0¾"
4-cyl. 2SCSA Doxford-type oil engine by Doxford and Sons (Engineers) Ltd., Sunderland; 670 x 2,320, 4,400 BHP, 12 knots.
29.12.1958: Launched by Sir James Laing and Sons Ltd., Sunderland (Yard No. 818) for Sheaf Steam Shipping Co. Ltd. (W.A. Souter and Co. Ltd., managers), Newcastle-upon-Tyne as SHEAF FIELD.
4.1959: Completed.
1969: Sold to Compania de Navigation Tornado SA, Panama (Societa Armamento in Nome Colletivo (SOARMA), Genoa, Italy) and renamed TORNADO under the Liberian flag.
1977: Sold to Greekhymne Shipping Co SA, Panama (Canopus Shipping SA (Andreas and George Kyrtatas, Piraeus, Greece) and renamed STENIES under the Greek flag.
25.5.1982: Laid up at Piraeus.
14.12.1986: Arrived at Aliaga from Piraeus for demolition by Nigdeliler AS.

The 'Sheaf' prefix and the title of the Sheaf Steam Shipping Co. Ltd. derives from the River Sheaf which runs through Sheffield where the company's founder, Sir William Souter, spent his childhood. SHEAF

Top to bottom: *Longstone* arriving at Newport on 27th April 1974, *Sheaf Field* in the Bristol Channel during June 1959, *Sheaf Wear* sailing from Birkenhead. *[J. and M. Clarkson]*

FIELD was the name given to the first ship that Sir William owned and this ore carrier was the fourth ship of the company to bear the name.

SHEAF WEAR 1959-1969

O.N. 186898 10,867g 5,761n 15,440d 503'5" x 70'0" x 28'0¾"
4-cyl. 2SCSA Doxford-type oil engine by William Doxford and Sons (Engineers) Ltd., Sunderland; 670 x 2,320, 4,400 BHP, 12 knots.
20.7.1959: Launched by Sir James Laing and Sons Ltd., Sunderland (Yard No. 821) for Sheaf Steam Shipping Co. Ltd. (W.A. Souter and Co. Ltd., managers), Newcastle-upon-Tyne as SHEAF WEAR.
11.1959: Completed.
1969: Sold to Whitwill Cole and Co. Ltd., Bristol (W.A. Souter and Co. Ltd.,

Newcastle-upon-Tyne, managers) and renamed BALTIC ORE.
1971: Renamed IRISH WASA.
1977: Sold to Universal Breeze Inc. (Stavros Daifas, Piraeus, Greece) and renamed CHRISTINA under the Greek flag.
14.2.1977: Abandoned by crew after fire and explosions five miles north of Corunna whilst on voyage from Glasgow to Ferrol in ballast. Towed into Ares Bay, in position 43.24 north by 08.15 west.
18.4.1977: Arrived at Bilbao for demolition by Hierros Ardos SA.

This ship was named after the River Wear where she was built and also Mrs R. Wear, the daughter of Sir William Souter.

FRENCH FLAG

LOUIS DREYFUS ET COMPAGNIE, PARIS.

PHILIPPE LD (PT) 1957-1974
O.N. 364080 6,733g 3,510n 9,310d
427'0" x 57'2" x 25'0"
Two 8-cyl. 4SCSA oil engines by
Klockner-Humboldt-Deutz, Köln,
geared to screw shaft; 420 x 660, 4,000
BHP, 12 knots.
3.11.1957: Launched by Société
Chantiers Reunis Loire-Normandie,
Grand Quévilly (Yard No. R308) for
Louis Dreyfus et Compagnie, Paris,
France as PHILIPPE LD.
1958: Completed.
1974: Sold to Salvesen Offshore
Holdings Ltd. (Christian Salvesen
(Managers) Ltd., managers) Edinburgh
and renamed SOUTRA.
1975: Renamed GULLANE.
11.1974 to 6.1976: Converted by North
East Coast Shiprepairers Ltd., South
Shields to a drillship and renamed
DALKEITH. Gross tonnage now
8,046. Converted to diesel-electric
propulsion, with four 16-cyl. 2SCSA
diesel engines by General Motors Corp,
La Grange, Illinois, USA, 230 x 254,
7,800 BHP, driving four 1,500kW
generators connected to four 1,000 BHP
electric motors geared to screw shafts.
1976: Renamed WINGATE for
duration of charter to City Drilling
Services Ltd.
1978: Renamed DALKEITH.
1980: Sold to JL Offshore Drilling Ltd.
(J. Lauritzen, manager), Copenhagen,
Denmark and renamed DAN BARON.
1981: Owners became Odin Shipping
Ltd., Hamilton, Bermuda (J. Lauritzen,
Copenhagen, Denmark) and placed
under the Bahamas flag.
1987: Sold to K/S Spectre Invest III
(Viking Offshore Drilling),
Kristiansand, Norway, and renamed
VIKING EXPLORER under the
Bahamas flag.
7.9.1988: Sank in the Makessar Strait
about 70 miles north east of Balikpaper
in position 00.46 south by 117.46 east
following a natural gas explosion.

Buries Markes Ltd., London

LA COLINA (PT) 1958-1974
O.N. 187793 7,216g, 3,391n 9,915d
427'0" x 57'2" x 25'0"
Two 8-cyl 4SCSA oil engines by
Klockner-Humboldt-Deutz, Köln,
geared to screw shaft; 420 x 660, 4,000
BHP, 12 knots.
6.3.1958: Launched by Société
Chantiers Reunis Loire-Normandie,
Grand Quévilly (Yard No. R309) for
Buries Markes Ltd., London as LA
COLINA.
1958: Completed.
1974: Sold to Prekookeanska Plovidba,
Bar, Yugoslavia and renamed
SUTOMORE.
1988: Sold to Incomn Ltd., London and

Phillipe LD leaving Port Talbot during September 1963. Note the bow. *[J. and M. Clarkson]*

Dalkeith. [World Ship Photo Library]

La Colina in June 1973. *[J. and M. Clarkson]*

renamed INCO 110 under the St.
Vincent flag.
5.2.1989: Arrived Alang having been
sold to International Steel Corporation,
Port Alang.

6.1989: Work began.

Buries Markes ships have names which
are Spanish words with the prefix La.
"Colina" is the Spanish word for hill.

NORWEGIAN FLAG

I/S FARLAND (SVERRE A FARSTAD AND CO, MANAGERS), AALESUND

FARLAND (PT) **1959-1970**
6,458g, 3,038n 10,510d 426'5" x 57'3" x 25'7³/4"
4-cyl. 2SCSA Gotaverken-type oil engines by Uddevallavarvet A/B, Uddevalla; 630 x 1,300, 3,350 BHP, 12 knots.
11.1959: Launched by Haugesund M/V A/S, Haugesund (Yard No. 18) for I/S Farland (Sverre A. Farstad and Co, managers), Aalesund, Norway as FARLAND.
1959: Completed.
1963: Sold to A/S Gerrards Rederi, Kristiansand, Norway and renamed GERLAND.
1970: Sold to Astramar Compania Argentiana de Navigacion SAC, Buenos Aires, Argentina and renamed ASTRANORTE.
26/27.9.1975: Struck reef and foundered in Fuigian Channel, southern tip of South America, whilst on voyage from Guayacan to San Nicolas, Argentina with a cargo of iron ore.

A/S GERRARDS REDERI, Kristiansand

GERORE (PT) **1959-1971**
6,665g 2,978n 10,650d 427'0" x 57'2" x 25'9¹/4"
Two 8-cyl. 4SCSA engines by Mirrlees, Bickerton and Day, Stockport geared to screw shaft; 425 x 450, 3,050 BHP, 12 knots.
1959: Completed by A/S Kristiansands M/V, Kristiansand (Yard No. 198) for A/S Gerrards Rederi, Kristiansand, Norway as GERORE.
1971: Sold to Gino Gardella SpA, Genoa, Italy and renamed LUIGI GARDELLA.
1988: Sold to St. Vincent flag owners and renamed GARD.
21.7.1988: Arrived Visakhapstan for demolition by Dhaka, Fouzderhat Beach, Bangladesh.
15.8.1988: Demolition commenced.

OLSEN AND UGELSTAD
A/S Falkefjell and A/S Dovrefjell (Olsen and Ugelstad, managers), Oslo

FILEFJELL (L) **1961-1967**
17,622g 8,656n 26,610d 605'0" x 80'2" x 32'0³/4"
6-cyl 2SCSA MAN-type oil engines by Kieler Howaldtswerke, Kiel; 780 x 1,400, 13 knots.
21.2.1961: Launched by Kieler Howaldtswerke, Kiel (Yard No. 1107) for A/S Falkefjell and A/S Dovrefjell (Olsen and Ugelstad, managers), Oslo, Norway as FILEFJELL.
1961: Completed.

Gerland. [John B. Hill collection]

Gerore in July 1963. [J. and M. Clarkson]

Filefjell in the Bristol Channel during November 1965. [J. and M. Clarkson]

1967: Sold to Ugland Shipping Co. A/S, Jorgensens R/A and S/A Kysten (Ugland Management Co. A/S), Grimstad, Norway and renamed NORITA.
1977: Owners became the Rodney Shipping Corporation, Monrovia (Ugland Management Co. A/S, Grimstad, Norway) and renamed ROSYTH.
28.4.1986: Arrived Kaohsiung for demolition by Tai Sheng Steel Co. Ltd.
8.5.1986: Work began.

B.J. RUUD-PEDERSEN
I/S Essex (B.J. Ruud-Pedersen, managers), Oslo

ESSEX (PT) 1958-1969
6,451g 3.031n 10,510d 505'0" x 57'3" x 25'7"
9-cyl 4SCSA oil engine by Maschinenbau Augsburg-Nurnberg, Augsburg; 520 x 740; 11 knots.
1.11.1958: Launched by Haugesund M/V A/S, Haugesund (Yard No. 17) for I/S Essex (B.J. Ruud-Pedersen, managers), Oslo, Norway as ESSEX.
1959: Completed.
1969: Converted to a bulk chemical (lead additive) tanker and renamed ESSI ANNE. Gross tonnage now 6,399.
1987: Sold to Ulyssis Shipping Co. Ltd., Malta and renamed E. ANNE for voyage to breakers.
30.11.1987: Arrived Karachi for demolition by Ahmed Maritime.

SIMONSEN AND ASTRUP
Victore Jenssens Rederi A/S (Simonsen and Alstrup, managers), Oslo

MESNA 1958-1968
10,649g 4,389n 16,000d 505'0" x 69'2" x 27'6"
7-cyl. 2SCSA engines by Maschinenbau Augsburg-Nurnberg, Augsburg; 700 x 1,200, 12.5 knots.
29.3.1958: Launched by N.V. Scheepswerf en Machinefabriek 'De Biesbosch', Dordrecht (Yard No. 364) for Victore Jenssens Rederi A/S (Simonsen and Alstrup, managers), Oslo, Norway as MESNA.
1958: Completed.
1968: Sold to Ugland Shipping Co. A/S, Jorgensens Rederi A/S and Skips A/S Kysten (Ugland Management Co. A/S), Grimstad, Norway and renamed BONITA.
1974: Owners became Short Trade Bulk Carriers Corporation, Liberia (Ugland Management Co. A/S, Grimstad, Norway) and renamed BONNYDALE.
1976: Sold to Compania Alecos SA, Panama (Dapo Shipping SA (N.A. Davaris and E. Pothitos), Piraeus, Greece) and renamed DAPO ALECOS.
7.11.1980: Sustained bottom damage during voyage from Port Cartier to Immingham.
8.11.1980: Beached at Mooring Cove.
13.2.1981: Refloated and later sold to owners given as Omnia Inc. and as Maria S. Shipping Co., Piraeus, Greece and renamed MARIA S.
22.6.1983: Left St. Johns, Newfoundland where she had been under arrest, in tow having been sold in damaged state to Desguaces Vige SA.
14.7.1983: Arrived at San Esteban de Pravia for demolition by Desguaces Vige SA.
19.8.1983: Work began.
She had not been repaired following her stranding in 1981.

Essex [David Whiteside collection]

Mesna in 1968. [J. and M. Clarkson]

Arabella. [J. and M. Clarkson]

M. CHR. STRAY
A/S Anatina (M. Chr. Stray, managers), Kristiansand

ARABELLA (PT) 1959-1974:
6,854g 3,522n 10,300d 427'0" x 57'3" x 25'9½"
5-cyl. 2SCSA B & W-type oil engines by Akers M/V., Oslo; 500 x 1,500, 11.5 knots.
8.1.1959: Launched by Moss Vaerft & Dock A/S, Moss (Yard No. 236) for A/S Anatina (M. Chr. Stray, managers), Kristiansand, Norway as ARABELLA.
1959: Completed.
1974: Sold to I/S Sunore (Olaf Pedersens Rederi A/S), Oslo, Norway and renamed SUNNY PRINCE.
1977: Sold to Sea Channel SA, Panama (Adamitron Ltd (F. Chapman), Rayleigh, Essex) and renamed SUNNY.
15.10.1985: Arrived at Split.
2.12.1985: Demolition began by Brodospas.

Carmencita sailing from Newport in April 1974. *[J. and M. Clarkson]*

J.M. UGLAND
A/S Uglands Rederij (J.M. Ugland, managers), Grimstad

CARMENCITA 1959-1975
10,858g 4,231n 16,300d 515'6" x 65'6" x 29'1½"
6-cyl. 2SCSA oil engines by A/B Gotaverken, Gothenburg; 680 x 1,500, 4,500 BHP, 13 knots.
14.5.1959: Launched by Oresundsvarvet A/B, Landskrona (Yard No. 166) for A/S Uglands Rederij (J.M. Ugland, managers), Grimstad, Norway as CARMENCITA.
8.1959: Completed.
1975: Owners became Short Trade Bulk Carriers Corporation, Liberia (Ugland Management Co. A/S, Grimstad, Norway) and renamed CARMENDALE.
1980: Sold to Galini Maritime Ltd. (Const. Tsamapoulos), Piraeus, Greece and renamed GALINI.
1.1983: Suffered a boiler explosion and engine room fire and subsequently laid up at Rotterdam.
5.1983: Arrived in tow at San Esteban de Pravia for demolition by Desguaces Aviles SA.
17.5.1983: Work began.

EVITA 1958-1972
10,859g 4,247n 16,250d 515'6" x 65'6" x 29'0¾"
6-cyl. 2SCSA oil engines by A/B Gotaverken, Gothenburg; 680 x 1,500, 4,500 BHP, 13 knots.
9.5.1958: Launched by Oresundsvarvet A/B, Landskrona (Yard No. 160) for A/S Uglands Rederij (J.M. Ugland, managers), Grimstad, Norway as EVITA.
9.1958: Completed.
1972: Owners became Short Trade Bulk Carriers Corporation, Liberia (Ugland Management Co. A/S, Grimstad, Norway) and renamed EVINDALE.
1978: Sold to Compania Antiklia SA, Panama (Dapo Shipping SA (N.A. Davaris), Piraeus, Greece and renamed DAPO ANTIKLIA.
1983: Renamed ANTIKLIA for voyage to breakers having been laid up at Galixidi from August 1982 to November 1983.
17.12.1983: Arrived at Port Alang for demolition by Gaziabad Shipbreakers.
31.1.1984: Demolition commenced.

Evita on 8th June 1970. *[J. and M. Clarkson]*

Favorita in the Bristol Channel during June 1960. *[J. and M. Clarkson]*

FAVORITA 1958-1973
10,858g 5,296n 16,582d 515'6" x 65'6" x 29'1½"
6-cyl. 2SCSA oil engine by A/B Gotaverken, Gothenburg; 680 x 1,500, 4,500 BHP, 13 knots.
20.11.1958: Launched by Oresundsvarvet A/B, Landskrona (Yard No. 161) for A/S Uglands Rederij (J.M. Ugland, managers), Grimstad, Norway as FAVORITA.
2.1959: Completed.
1973: Owners became Short Trade Bulk Carriers Corporation, Liberia (Ugland Management Co. A/S, Grimstad, Norway) and renamed FALCONDALE.
1976: Sold to Atlantic Minerals Transport Corporation, Monrovia, Liberia (Amax Inc., Greenwich, Connecticut, USA) and renamed AMAX MINER.
1980: Sold to Dimona Shipping Corporation, Panama (Aslak International Inc., Piraeus, Greece) and renamed MARTHA L.
23.4.1982: Laid up at Bilbao.
30.12.1983: Arrived Santander from Bilbao for demolition by SA Desbar.

VESTERAALENS D/S, STOKMARKNES

NORDLAND 1958-1972
10,707g 5,893n 16,400d 505'0" x 64'0" x 30'1¾"
4-cyl. 2SCSA Doxford-type oil engine by Marinens Hovedverft, Horten; 670 x 2,320, 12.5 knots.
26.4.1958: Launched by Kaldnes M/V A/S, Tonsberg (Yard No. 144) for Vesteraalens D/S, Stokmarknes, Norway as NORDLAND.
26.12.1972: Badly damaged by fire which broke out in the engine room whilst lying at Rotterdam. She was subsequently sold in a damaged state to Good Trader Navigation Co. Ltd., Nicosia, Cyprus (N. Frangos and N. and M. Moundreas, Piraeus, Greece) and renamed GOOD TRADER.
1975: Sold to Bretha Segunda Shipping SA, Panama (Rea Shipping Agency Co. SA., Piraeus, Greece) and renamed MALESSINA under the Greek flag.
1981: Sold to Loydias Compania Naviera SA, Panama (Golden Union Shipping Co. SA (Theodoros E. Veniamis), Piraeus, Greece) and renamed DELTA FLAG under the Greek flag.
1985: Converted to cement storage vessel.
1.2.1992: Arrived at Aliaga in tow from Greece for demolition by Leyal Gemi Sokum Ticaret AS.

Nordland. [J. and M. Clarkson]

MISFORTUNES OF WAR
Photographs from David Hodge

David Hodge has very kindly allowed *Record* to reproduce these fascinating photographs taken during the First World War from Royal Naval Airships C23A and C9 based at Mullion. The commentaries are based on David's research, with biographical details of the ships taken from the Registers of Bill Schell and Richard and Bridget Larn's 'Shipwreck Index of the British Isles', volume 1. They are poignant reminders of loss and danger in wartime, and may also be some of the earliest aerial photographs of merchant shipping.

Taken at 12.10 on 19th November 1917, the photographs below give one an uneasy feeling of witnessing one of the many tragedies of the First World War at sea. They show the French steamer *Saint Andre* (2,457/1907) soon after she had been torpedoed by *UB 58* south west of the Eddystone. Floating clear is her cargo of empty barrels which she was carrying from Rouen to Algiers. The barrels may still be keeping her afloat, as she later sank. *Saint Andre* had been built at Dunkerque, and at the time of her loss was owned by Société Navale de l'Ouest, Havre.

Above: The wreck of the *Corvus* (570/1908) is a reminder that wrecks and strandings were even more likely in wartime, with lights extinguished. The Norwegian steamer had been taken over from Det Bergenske Dampskibselskab by the Shipping Controller in 1917, and was being managed by Everett and Newbiggin of Newcastle-upon-Tyne. In fog on the morning of 22nd March 1918 she was wrecked on Stag Rocks, near the Lizard whilst on a voyage from Swansea to Rouen with a coal cargo. Airship C23A photographed her at 11.15 the day after the wreck. *Corvus* had been built at Fredrikstad for another Bergen owner as *Königsberg*.

Right: On 2nd May 1918, the Tønsberg-owned *Norlands* (1,272/1888) was wrecked near Godrevy Lighthouse, three miles off St. Ives Head, whilst on a voyage from Swansea to Rouen with coal. This photograph of the wreck was taken on 8th May by Royal Naval Airship C9. The crew of *Norlands* had been rescued by the St. Ives Lifeboat soon after the stranding.

The old ship had been built as *Salerno* by Osbourne, Graham and Co., Sunderland for Scrutton, Sons and Co., London. She carried the name *Hogland* in Swedish ownership from 1897 to 1911, when sold to A/S Norland (A. Monsen, manager) and renamed *Norlands*.

The *Motagua* (6,014/1912) was a victim of a form of 'friendly fire'. On 20th March 1918, the armed merchant cruiser was returning to Plymouth from escort duty when she passed rather too close to the destroyer USS *Manley*. The swell lifted *Motagua*'s stern on to the destroyer's quarter, exploding depth charges which caused the damage seen in the photograph, in which *Motagua* is being towed into Plymouth.

The Swan, Hunter-built reefer had been bought by Elders and Fyffes Ltd. in March 1914 from Hamburg-Amerika Linie, who had run her as *Emil L. Boas*. As *Motagua* she lasted until broken up at Hendrik-ido-Ambacht in 1933.

From ships which were recently casualties, to one which was about to become one. Just hours, or perhaps even minutes, after this photograph was taken on 10th March 1918, the *Cristina* (2,042/1903) was torpedoed by *U 55* three miles off St. Agnes, despite her highly visible Spanish neutrality markings. She was on a voyage from Port Talbot to Bilbao.

The steamer was owned by Compania Naviera Vascongada of Bilbao and had been built in Spain as *Cadiz 2*, becoming *Kiora* for Trechmann Brothers of West Hartlepool, before returning to the Spanish flag as *Cristina* in 1914.

MAGDALENA: TRIALS AND TRAGEDY
Photographs from Arthur Bower

Magdalena shared with the *Titanic* the unhappy fate of being lost on a peacetime maiden voyage. The splendid photographs of her steaming at 20.25 knots off a wintry Isle of Arran (above) and returning to Belfast on their completion on 17th February 1949 (below) contrast only too starkly with the broken hulk seen lying off Rio de Janeiro a little over two months later, on 29th April (opposite).

Royal Mail Lines ordered the *Magdalena* from Harland and Wolff Ltd. to replace the *Highland Patriot* (14,157/1932), lost in October 1940. Despite being designed to run with the five surviving ex-Nelson Line motorships, *Magdalena* had Parson's turbines driving twin screws. Her Foster Wheeler boilers were designed to produce at 525 pounds per square inch and superheated to 825 degrees Fahrenheit, but were by no means trouble free, as witness the black smoke pouring from the funnel on her return to Belfast.

Magdalena and the Highland ships ran a service somewhat secondary to that carrying the mail from Southampton to Rio de Janeiro, Montevideo and Buenos Aires and in the hands of *Andes* and *Alcantara*. *Magdalena* was to run from Tilbury and make additional calls at Pernambuco and Bahia.

Early on the morning of 25th April, on the homeward leg of her first voyage home from Buenos Aires, *Magdalena* ran on to the Tijucas Rocks, south of Rio de Janeiro. All the passengers were taken off safely. The double-bottom tanks were pierced, but only number 3 hold was flooded: number 2 was making water but was under control. Prospects for salvage seemed good, and indeed *Magdalena* was towed off stern first the following morning at high water. However, whilst being towed into Rio harbour, the bow which was drawing 45 feet of water touched bottom off Fort São João in the swell, and *Magdalena* broke apart just forward of the superstructure. The stern portion was beached in Imbui Bay, as seen above, and was soon abandoned as a total loss. At the time, her insured value of £2 million represented the largest marine loss ever, twice the insured value of the *Titanic*. Only £50,000 was recovered from the sale of the stern part for scrap. At the subsequent inquiry, Captain D.R. Lee accepted full responsibility for the accident.

Harland and Wolff got excited twice, first at the prospect of building a new forepart for *Magdalena*, and after she was abandoned at the chances of an order for a replacement. But their hopes were dashed by Royal Mail chairman Walter C. Warwick, who used the company's AGM in June 1949 to bewail the high cost of shipbuilding, and to firmly indicate that their existing ships would have to suffice. It was to be almost ten years before the builders got their orders for the *Amazon*, *Aragon* and *Arlanza* to replace the Highland ships. In many ways, and especially with their split superstructure, their design echoed that of the ill-fated *Magdalena*.

Arthur Bower's father, Arthur Bower MBE, was *Magdalena*'s Chief Electrical Engineer, standing by the ship at Belfast and surviving her loss only because he was a strong swimmer.

SOURCES AND ACKNOWLEDGEMENTS
Photographs are from the collection of John Clarkson unless otherwise credited. We thank all who gave permission for their photographs to be used, and for help in finding photographs we are particularly grateful to Tony Smith, Jim McFaul and David Whiteside of the World Ship Photo Library; to Ian Farquhar, Bill Laxon, Peter Newall, Ivor Rooke, William Schell, George Scott; to David Hodge and Bob Todd of the National Maritime Museum; Dr. David Jenkins of the National Museums and Galleries of Wales; and other museums and institutions listed.

Research sources have included the *Registers* of William Schell and Tony Starke, *Lloyd's Register*, *Lloyd's Confidential Index*, *Lloyd's War Losses*, *Mercantile Navy Lists*, and *Marine News*. Use of the facilities of the World Ship Society's Central Record, the Guildhall Library, the Public Record Office and Lloyd's Register of Shipping are gratefully acknowledged. Particular thanks also to William Schell and John Bartlett for various information, to Heather Fenton for editorial and indexing work, and to Marion Clarkson for accountancy services.

The Iron Ladies
Inevitably on an exercise like this the author's task has been to pull together information supplied by many others, and Bernard McCall and Ian Buxton are particularly thanked for acting almost as mentors. Other people who have assisted with this project include D.V. Cameron, former Chief Marine Superintendent of the British Steel Corporation, L.G. Fryer and K.G. Partridge of Marine Agencies Ltd, John B. Hill, Dennis Johnzon, Ron Mapplebeck and Mike Ridgard.

Derick Goubert - Captain/owner
Many thanks to Captain Derick Goubert and Roy South, his chartering manager at Everards, for talking to the author and sharing their memories with him during the preparation of this article.

Those old iron hulls
Reference has been made to Kenneth Brown, 'Stadium, ex-Beechdale - barque, hulk, motorship', *Sea Breezes* (New Series), Vol. 14, 1952, pp.320-2 and to information supplied by Mike Cooper and Fulvio Petronio.

Photographer in Focus: Cliff Parsons
Thanks to Clive Guthrie for help identifying the location of the photograph of *Cadishead*.

Sunderland in Focus 2
The 1960s aerial photograph was taken, and supplied, by George Taylor, who also supplied the series of aerial photographs taken in 1930. The 1979 view of the Austin & Pickersgill shipyard is from the Author's collection. Reference to books written by Sawyer and Mitchell, MacRae and Waine, N.L Middlemiss, Paul Heaton, J.H. Proud and P.N. Thomas, together with various World Ship Society publications is acknowledged.

THOSE OLD IRON HULLS
John Naylon

No better instance could be cited of the proverbial durability and longevity of nineteenth-century iron sailing ships' hulls than the barque *Beechdale* which, in one form or another, lasted some 93 years. Three photographs kindly provided by Mike Cooper, from the collection of Fulvio Petronio, Trieste, illustrate her remarkable career.

The *Beechdale* was launched in February 1877 by the well-known Liverpool shipbuilders W.H. Potter and Co., who later built the four-masted barque *Wanderer*, made famous by John Masefield. Potters had their yard on the Mersey foreshore at Baffin Street, between the Queen's Half-Tide Dock and Coburg Dock. Yard No. 68 was built for E.E. Broomhall, a ships' stores dealer and wine merchant of Redcross Street, Liverpool, who also owned the composite barque *Tarapaca* (1862/493gt, 150.8 feet) and the composite ship *Hoang Ho* (1864/565gt, 170.0 feet), which traded to the west coast of South America. The *Beechdale* was bigger at 815gt and 792nt on dimensions 192.2 x 30.7 x 19.2 feet. Her official number was 76485 and her signal letters DNJT.

On 28th August 1892 the *Beechdale* was bought by Enrico Angelo Jasbitz, Piazza della Corsa 14, Trieste, who operated her under the Austrian flag for 19 years without changing her name (her signal letters became HCTB). Trieste was at that time the main port of the Austro-Hungarian empire and was characterized by mostly small individual and family shipowners who, as in Italy, went in for considerable buying of second-hand British and American tonnage. Thus Jasbitz also owned the iron screw steamer *Kate*, ex-*Kingsdale*, 2,224gt, launched in July 1883 by Short Bros. of Sunderland.

Pictured here at Trieste soon after her purchase, the *Beechdale* was the typical iron barque of her time. With an unbroken sheerline from bow to taffrail - the raised quarterdeck (37 feet long in the *Beechdale*'s case) being flush with the rail - these were some of the prettiest models ever launched. As they became too small for world-wide trading, many of them went out to the colonies or to the Mediterranean.

The *Beechdale*'s sailing days ended on 24th July 1911 when she was taken over by the Österreichischen Lloyd company, also of Trieste, who reduced her to a hulk, renamed her *Stadium* and moored her in Trieste harbour as a floating store and explosives depot.

After the First World War and the transfer of Trieste to Italy, the hulk was purchased by Prima Spremitura de Olio and converted to a barge for the transport of bulk oil and oil seed to and from Trieste and Luzzatti & Co.'s oil mill at Monfalcone, some 20 miles across the Gulf of Trieste.

Just prior to the outbreak of the Second World War in 1939, during a periodic survey, the owners' attention was drawn to the excellent state of preservation of the hull and they decided to rebuild the *Stadium* as a cargo motorship. The war interrupted these plans but work was resumed in 1946, shipping tonnage being scarce, and completed in 1948. Reconstruction was carried out to the highest class of the Registro Navale Italiano, the Italian classification society. The length of the hull was reduced by nearly 50 feet, giving new dimensions of

145.5 x 30.0 x 10.5 feet, new tonnages of 927 gross and 704 net, and a deadweight capacity of 1,270 tons. The net tonnage was reduced by the fitting of a 600hp oil engine built by Burmeister & Wain at Copenhagen in 1943, giving a speed of over 10 knots.

Emerging as a modern-looking motorship, the *Stadium* continued in the ownership of Prima Spremitura till 1959, when she was sold to Balducci SpA, passing later to Mancino Salvatore of Naples. Employed in the Near East and Red Sea trades, she was not scrapped until 1970 - a tribute to the Merseyside builders' workmanship.

POETRY CORNER

The query from Dr. David Jenkins in *Record* 23 about the 'Doxford ditty', sung by engineers to the tune of 'McNamara's Band', has elicited further verses, and indeed further versions, of this entertainment. Captain A.W. Kinghorn recalls the following performed aboard the *Adelaide Star.*

1. You must have heard of Charlie Parsons, and Doctor Sulzer too.
   You all know of the M.A.N and the B. and W.
   But the best marine propulsion, I'm sure you will agree,
   Comes from a place called Sunderland, where it's made by William D.

   Chorus:
   Oh me name is William Doxford, I come from Sunderland.
   They say I build the finest engines made in all the land.
   The top ends clang, the bottom ends bang, the engine clangs away.
   You've only got to stop my engine every - other - day.

2. The chiefs and seconds and thirds and fourths who take my ships to sea,
   They all are very happy, they all are proud of me.
   They all declare that William Doxford's engine stands alone,
   (They all work 24 hours a day to keep the b-----d going.)

3. Well, the captain stands upon his bridge, his mind is quite at rest.
   He knows that with his Doxford engine he has got the best.
   He turns to sparks and says to him, 'Let's send an ETA.'
   (The only things they can't put on it are the date and day.)

4. We've crossed the broad Pacific, and the Panama Canal.
   I think we'll get to Liverpool - in fact I'm *sure* we shall.
   The engineers have sweated tears from Bluff to Curacao,
   But we have got two Doxfords, which DIVVENT WANT TO GO!

5. We're drifting across the Pacific, as happy as happy can be,
   Everyone's singing the praises of Sunderland's William D.
   We're rolling across the Atlantic at a comfortable nine and a half.
   The Old Man is going quite frantic - while the passengers try not to laugh. [Because the longer their ride, the cheaper the fare.]

6. Well, a quarter century has passed, it's time for her to die.
   She's going to Masan at last, and home from there we'll fly.
   They'll make her into razorblades and stereophonic gear,
   But evermore this phantom song will haunt them in Korea

7. Oh, my namee William Doxford, I live in Sunderland.
   They say I makee finest engine made in allee land.
   Top end clang, bottom end clang, engine clang away.
   CANNOT STOPPEE DOXFORD ENGINE, ANY DOXFORD WAY!

Other versions have survived, and one which appeared on the Internet has been submitted by George Ball, Michael Pryce and Tom Scott. This comes with instructions. At a party six females (preferably) would be numbered 1 to 6. With their hands on heads and with elbows sticking out (to imitate the Doxford piston's transverse beam), the conductor would get them to bob up and down in the firing order that he called, to replicate the action of the engine. In the chorus, the performers placed two clenched fists in front of their faces, vertically one above the other, and at the words Chuff! Chuff! pulled them apart to imitate an opposed piston action. If anyone has a video of this, please send it to the editors in a plain wrapper.

1. Oh my name is William Doxford and I come from Sunderland,
   They say my diesel engine is the finest in the land.
   The pistons bang, the cranks go clang and the camshaft grinds away,
   And it's the bestest engine you could hear about today.

   Chorus
   Dah dah dah dah Chuff! Chuff! Dah dah dah dah Chuff! Chuff!
   Dah dah dah dah Chuff! Chuff! Dah dah dah dah.
   Dah dah dah dah Chuff! Chuff! Dah Dah Dah - Dah
   With action and reaction we'll go sailing on our way.

2. To see our engine's functionals we open up a door,
   We find more cranks and crossheads than we've ever seen before.
   And then we pull the pistons out to calibrate the bore.
   And here for us to work on there are piston rings galore.

3. We calculate the horsepower by scientific means
   With bits of string and paper wound on little round machines.
   We measure round the diagrams the power it should tell,
   The outcome's automatic but the engine's aw 'ta hell.

In both versions the words fit 'McNamara's Band', but Mr. A. Frost (who claims to have witnessed Captain Kinghorn performing the song on his squeeze box) thinks this tune would have Geordies choking on their Brown Ale, and suggests the right song was 'Blaydon Races'. The Performing Arts Critic of *Record* has reservations about his, especially as it is a Tyneside song; surely any self-respecting Wearsider would have used 'The Lambton Worm'? The sentiments, at least, of most of Mr. Scott's verses are similar to those above, but he brings the ditty up-to-date:

To all you engineer cadets that go to sea
Who do not know the engine made by William D.
Because there are now only two,
The Sulzer and the B and double U!

Who says marine engineers haven't got poetry in their souls?

The inspiration: a four-cylinder Doxford opposed-piston oil engine.
[National Museums and Galleries of Wales].

PUTTING THE RECORD STRAIGHT

Letters, additions, amendments and photographs relating to articles in any issues of *Record* are welcomed. Letters may be lightly edited. E-mails are welcome, but senders are asked to include their postal address.

So it's all down hill from here, then?
This is an unabashed fan letter. The interest and quality in *Record* No 24 scales new heights of excellence. Including the GA from 'Shipbuilding and Marine Engine Builder' of the Big Ics ensured that the article will long be a work of reference for many, for years to come.

The way in which 'Old Wine, New Bottles' compares the ships' after-lives, even taken from the same angles, is masterly and the quality of the printing just about as good as it could ever be.

If I was a real-life cynic I would advise you to quit while you are ahead and never produce another edition.
ANDREW BELL, Gartul, Porthleven, Helston, Cornwall TR13 9JJ

The engineer's finger
What a cracking article/photographs in *Record* 24 on the 'Sam Boat' engine room and, my word, did it bring the memories flooding back. I could almost feel the heat and smell the steam and hot oil!

The posed photo of oiler (greaser in Merchant Navy parlance of course!) Ralph Ahlgren checking the bottom-end bearing temperature reminded me of the first time I was shown and subsequently used this technique on Brocklebanks *Maihar* of 1917.

It was 1960 and my first time on an 'up-and-downer'. I was on the 12 to 4 watch with the Third Engineer, standing beside this symphony of majestically revolving machinery, and, when he explained what we were about to do, I thought, 'Ah-ah he's taking the Mickey (like when you are sent to the stores when you are an apprentice and told to ask for 'a long stand') and when I've nearly lost my hand he'll fall about laughing and tell me I've been got!'

However, when I saw him do it first, to show me what to do, it dawned on me that it was for real and I was going to have to do it too!

The first attempt was quite nerve-wracking and I bottled, which was quite dangerous as you have to keep your fingers absolutely arrow-straight when you introduce them between the bottom-end and crank web to touch the bottom-end journal but the Third was a very experienced engineer and understood my fears and went through the procedure several times until I plucked up the courage to try once again with great success. Once I'd mastered it I felt quite euphoric and did it over and over again until the Third told me that people had suffered broken arms by becoming too cocky when they were 'feeling round' so it didn't do to become too complacent! Plus, he told me, if anyone had been working on the bearings and fitted shims without making certain they had been well trimmed back the sure-fire result would be badly lacerated fingers for the first person to check the bottom-ends for temperature and oil-film, once the engine was turning.

So thank you very much for getting the nostalgia flowing again and congratulations on a wonderful article/photographs.
PHIL ROE, 29, Roman Avenue South, Stamford Bridge, York YO41 1EZ

Relocating *Ulidia*
In *Record* 22, page 126, *Ulidia* is described as 'Probably in an Eastern Mediterranean port'. I would hardly think so; the craft on the right are both of Dutch origin, the larger being a tjalk. I would say Rotterdam.
PETER HERBERT, 'Godrevy', 5 Greenacre Close, Northam, Bideford EX39 1DA
His many friends will be saddened to learn that Peter Herbert died late in June. Our condolences to Peter's family.

Rosetta Maru opens Nagoya
The *Rosetta Maru* (*Record* 23, page 151) called at the port of Nagoya, one year ahead of its opening. At that time the local government in charge of Nagoya earnestly wished for it to be approved by the Central Government as an official open sea port.

S. Okuda, Director of the port, asked the captain of the *Rosetta Maru* to call at the port as the ship was one of the largest ships in Japan to show that the port was worthy of being an official open port.

Okuda promised to act as pilot as the captain was reluctant to call at the port that was then unknown even on the chart. At last, the *Rosetta Maru* successfully entered the port.

With this incident, the port of Nagoya was finally designated as an official open sea port in the following year of 1907.
Letter from MASHIKO KATO, Nagoya Maritime Museum, Nagoya 455, Japan kindly forwarded by ANNE COWNE, Lloyd's Register of Shipping.

Ore carriers and Big Ics
John Harrison's articles on ore carriers have been very well received, and comments and additions to these (several received just as we were going to press) have been held over until the next issue to be consolidated with any arising from the third part of the feature.

We have also had a positive response to requests for photographs of Shaw, Savill's Ceramic and Gothic in pre-Thornycroft funnel days, and will include these in the next issue. Ed.

Explaining the *White Jacket*
The explanation of the hidden raised quarter deck of the *White Jacket* (*Record* 23, page 182) is to be found in the description of 'Types of vessels' in 'Lloyd's Registers' of the early twentieth century. She was a 'part awning deck vessel having forecastle and bridge combined, with raised quarter deck and poop.' The sketch below explains the deck levels. The wash ports above the quarter deck are visible in the photograph.

Presumably this design was seeking favourable tonnage measurement of the kind enjoyed by the Doxford Turret steamer and the shade-decked vessel.
JOHN BARTLETT, 6 Cottenham Park Road, London SW20 0AZ

"PART AWNING DECK VESSEL." VESSEL HAVING FORECASTLE AND BRIDGE COMBINED WITH RAISED QUARTER DECK AND POOP.

POOP. RAISED QUARTER DECK. PART AWNING DECK.

Additions and corrections

For *Record* 23 I can add the following Bergen Line launch dates:

Page 133: *Vega* launched 9th March 1895; *Irma* launched 5th January 1905.

Page 134: *Leda* launched 4th May 1920.

Page 140: *Leda* launched 3rd September 1952.

Page 141: *Meteor* launched 6th May 1954.

Page 142: *Jupiter* launched 5th March 1966, and *Black Prince* launched 14th May 1966.

Page 136: It's a pity that a photo of *Venus* in her original pre-war guise wasn't able to be included.

Page 145: *Empire* had only 15, not 18, years service with Eastern and Australian. She was sold in 1917 to R.L. Connell of Liverpool without change of name. I think he might have been a stooge for the Compagnie Generale Transatlantique, to which she was sold in 1920 and renamed *Volubilis*.

Page 145: *Kyarra's* engines were by Denny and Co. The hull and engine builders were not combined into the one company until 1918.

Page 154: I found the first instalment of 'The Iron Ladies' very interesting. I endorse the editorial comments.

Page 176: *Drechtdijk*: Surely Operation Sealion had been abandoned by March 1941. Should the date not be one in 1940? - see the text for *Damsterdijk* on Page 179.

Record 24, Page 215: *Cape Nelson*: The breakers of this ship were in Colombia, not Columbia.

Page 242: *Puriri*: The photograph does not show her in New Zealand Shipping Company colours. Like her four other ex-German dry cargo consorts in the Federal fleet, she has a plain black, rather than a yellow funnel. Refer to 'Crossed Flags' page 128.

Page 244: *Shahristan's* German name from 1913 was *Ninive*, not *Niniva*.

I enjoyed Malcolm Cooper's account of Skinner's Castles very much. Here are one or two extra pieces of information.

Page 254: *Edinburgh Castle* was launched 16.5.1863.

Page 255: *Huntly Castle* as *Atiet Rohoman* was reported as being 'in port, damaged' in January 1898.

Page 256: *Norham Castle* was launched 30.4.1869.

Page 257: *Gordon Castle*: Neil McLean and Co. were placed in liquidation in 1896.

Loudon Castle was broken up at Savona (in 1923).

Page 258: *Bothwell Castle* was launched on 1.3.1881.

Page 259: *Stirling Castle's* 1900 rebuilding and re-engining were carried out by Palmers at Newcastle.

Minard Castle was launched 21.12.1881.

BILL LAXON, Waimarama, Upper Whangateau Road, PO Box 171, Matakana 1240, New Zealand.

A photograph of the Venus *of 1931 in original condition did appear in the first part of Anthony Cooke's Bergen Line article in* Record 22. *The date for* Drechtdijk's *conversion to an Operation Sealion transport should certainly have been August 1940. We thank Bob Todd and David Hodge of the National Maritime Museum for also pointing this out. Ed.*

Sulaco (*Record* 24, page 247) was lost on 20th October 1940 in OB.228 not on 20th October 1943 in HX.228. *U 124* (which was the U-boat responsible) was actually sunk on 4th April 1943 and HX.228 was at sea in March of that year.
MALCOLM COOPER, Flat 5, Leonard Court, 68 Westbourne Terrace, London W2 3UF

One small, but to me important, correction to Anthony Cooke's article about the Bergen Line (*Records* 22 and 23). He writes that the *Jupiter/Black Watch* were on the summer carferry/passenger service to the Tyne and Rotterdam. Actually, the summer services have always been to Amsterdam. Winter cruising and Canary Islands services have always been from Rotterdam, although lately Fred. Olsen's cruising is done solely from Amsterdam/Ijmuiden.
CHRIS F. KLEISS, Sparrendaal 22, 1187 KG Amstelveen, The Netherlands

Tanker to ferry in two stages

Frank Heine, my co-author of the 'Tanker to Ferry' articles which appeared in *Records* 17 and 18, has pointed out that *Efthycosta II* went through two transitions in her layout as a vehicle carrier. We have now seen a photograph in a back copy of the Greek shipping magazine 'Efoplistis' which confirms that the lowermost picture on page 30 of *Record* 17 represents the first stage of conversion in which the amidships superstructure was altered only to the extent that a single passage for trucks was created just off the centreline on the main deck. The middle picture on page 30 shows the *Efthycosta II* undergoing a second stage of conversion to the form where most of the width of the main deck is available for vehicles beneath the bridge superstructure. We presume that her re-naming as *Zakros* would have been imminent, although this still does not explain why she appears to be sporting a dark funnel colour (since every other photograph we possess shows her with a white funnel).
ROLAND WHAITE, 9 The Paddock, Chepstow, Monmouthshire NP16 5BW

Liveries lived on

Record 24 is very interesting - I liked the feature 'Old wine, new bottles'. I can confirm that all the Moss Hutchison ships that were taken over in the October 1971 revolution retained their original colours - *Amarna, Assiout, Kypros, Melita, Makaria* and *Tabor*. The two Ms were the last to go, in 1979. Nice to see the photo of *Bulimba* - I was involved in the design of the B class when in the British India Drawing Office, and always thought that they looked particularly well. Regarding the passing of the old company's livery in 1971, B.I. kept their old colours on *Karanja, Dwarka, Dumra* and *Uganda*, together with the 'Old faithful' *Rajula*, until they were scrapped or sold.
TONY SMYTHE, 35 Avondale Road, Rayleigh Essex SS6 8NJ

As Tony Smythe indicates, *Amarna* of 1949 defied P&O's strictures on corporate identity and remained in Moss Hutchinson's classic livery until sold to Grecomar Shipping in 1975. She became *Kastriani*, keeping this name until demolished at Gadani Beach in 1984. Her photograph is a reminder that *Record* has hardly touched on Moss Hutchinson: is there anyone out there who could, for instance, write about their post-war ships? Photographs are not a problem. [*Roy Fenton collection*]

PUTTING 'FEILDEN'S MERSEY' STRAIGHT

Published in late 2001, 'Feilden's Mersey' is an album containing 127 of what the publishers believed were some of the best of Basil Feilden's post-war images. Captions were purposely brief to maximise the area available for photographs, and also because the book was aimed not only at enthusiasts but also at Merseyside locals who might recall some of the ships featured. However, in the Ships in Focus tradition, we confess our sins of omission and commission in the compiling of the captions, readers having kindly taken the trouble to point these out to us.

Our most embarrassing sin was to confuse the pre- and post-Second World War ships named *Cyprian Prince*. Our excuse is that we believed all the negatives, which had recently been acquired by John Clarkson, were taken post-war. Indeed, this was our reason for choosing photographs from this period, as the images had not been available since Basil himself had printed from them. However, the *Cyprian Prince* we illustrated on page 20 was the 1937-built vessel of this name, completed by the Furness Shipbuilding Co. Ltd. of Haverton Hill-on-Tees, of 1,988gt and 296 feet overall. She had a triple-expansion steam engine by Richardsons, Westgarth and Co. Ld., West Hartlepool. This *Cyprian Prince*, the third of the name, was lost on 10th April 1941 during the German air attacks on Piraeus. Above we illustrate the real post-war *Cyprian Prince*. The 1949 motor vessel has a profile not dissimilar to the earlier ship of the name, albeit she is somewhat larger and has a larger superstructure.

Pages 10 and 11 devoted to Elder, Dempster ships have provoked much comment. In *Aureol*'s caption we expressed surprise that she and the other mail ships were not equipped with air conditioning until 1961. Andrew Bell notes that there is much correspondence in the archives of builders Alexander Stephen and Sons Ltd. concerning air conditioning the whole ship, but this was not done because of post-war shortages. All three ships were built so that air conditioning could be installed, and this was eventually done between voyages.

Andrew also comments on our blaming air travel for the withdrawal of *Apapa*. In fact, she and *Accra* could break even on cargo alone, and it was a case of it not being worth putting the two ships through their special surveys because their hulls were of poor quality steel. The pair were replaced by two of the *Fourah Bay* class motorships.

Andrew Bell and John B. Hill point out that *Onitsha*, with her 150-ton derrick, was not merely countering competition from specialist heavy-lift ships, but maintaining a service already established by the *Mary Kingsley* of 1930. Elder, Dempster always aimed to have one heavy lift ship in the fleet.

The 1949-built *Cyprian Prince*. As recorded in 'Feilden's Mersey', she was sold after 18 years' Prince Line service and carried the names *Agios Dionisios*, *Irene's Wish*, and *Fulmartrader*. In January 1976 she was abandoned in the Mediterranean when a fire broke out in her engine room. She was first towed into Palma, from where she was taken in tow for Piraeus but sank off Palermo on 14th February. [World Ship Photo Library]

David Edge points out that following her sale the *Apapa* was employed as *Taipooshan* on Shun Cheong's liner service from Hong Kong to Penang via Singapore. She looked smart in Shun Cheong's colours with a white hull and yellow funnel with red, white and blue bands.

We ought to have been counting masts more carefully, as *Warwickshire* on page 12 is described as having changed Bibby's profile, coming down from four masts to one. In fact, as Paul Boot and David Edge point out, she clearly has two masts: it was her sister *Leicestershire* that had only one.

Andrew Bell qualifies the statement in the caption to *Astyanax* (page 14) that Alfred Holts carried their own insurance. In fact, they had a policy with Lloyds which would pay out if they had two constructive total losses in one year. Andrew adds that such was Blue Funnel and Glen Line's record that the policy was very cheaply written.

Commenting on the caption to Harrison's *Journalist* on page 17, Adam Softley notes that the company introduced their new profile with the *Astronomer* of 1951. Their twelve engines-amidships vessels built by Doxfords had two heavy-lift derricks, commencing with one 60-ton and one 40-ton derrick on the first four, and finishing with two 70-ton derricks on the final three. The *Journalist* had one 70-ton and one 60-ton derrick.

Scottish Star (page 22) and *Port Victor* (page 40) were both twin screw.

Paul Boot reckons we were wrong to describe *Armanistan* on page 34 as sailing from Manchester, and thinks she was photographed off Gladstone Dock.

We got our British wartime standard ships in twist. *Hesperides* on page 25 has a full-height poop and is a 'D' class. *Waynegate* on page 44 is a 'C' type with a half-height poop. Regarding the comments under *Fort Sturgeon* about distinguishing between the Empire 'B' type and 'Forts' and 'Parks', David Edge points that the 'B' type had a raised forecastle and no sheer over the length of the holds. This was true for most of the 'B's, but inspection of Mitchell and Sawyer's 'The Empire Ships' reveals a number of British-built standard ships, ostensibly of the 'B' type, with no forecastle and similar sheer to the Canadian-built ships.

Adam Softley points out that the *Southern Harvester* (page 78) and her sister *Southern Venturer* were twin-screw ships, propelled by two triple-expansion engines. We followed 'Lloyd's Register's' lead in citing the total number of cylinders fitted.

Despite these few blemishes, 'Feilden's Mersey' has been well received by our customers. Copies of this 80-page landscape-format softback are still available from our Preston address at a very reasonable £8.00 plus postage.

One of Elder, Dempster's 'Explorer' class, *Mary Kingsley* had two 100-ton derricks mainly to carry locomotives. Built by Ardrossan Dockyard Ltd. in 1930, the 4,017gt motorship was given a Burmeister & Wain type diesel built by J.G. Kincaid and Co. Ltd. A breakdown in this engine in 1952 seems to have signalled the end of her career, and she was laid up at Dartmouth. She was broken up by T.W. Ward Ltd. at Preston where she arrived on 18th September 1954. *[J. and M. Clarkson]*

Elder, Dempster's *Apapa* as *Taipooshan* at anchor probably in Hong Kong harbour; note the passengers boarding from the boat by the ladder. Owners were Shung Cheong Steam Navigation Co. Ltd. of

Hong Kong. *Taipooshan* arrived at Kaohsiung for breaking up on 23rd February 1975. *[A. Duncan]*

VERY LOOSE ENDS: AUSTRALIND

This is the loosest of loose ends, as it relates to the inaugural issue of *Record* back in 1996, when our first Fleet in Focus featured the Australind Steam Shipping Co. Ltd. Photographs of two Australind's ships could not be found, but nil desperandum: Ian Farquhar has very kindly provided shots of both. A few copies of *Record* 1 including the Australind feature are still available from Ships in Focus (see inside front cover).

ATHOLL (upper)

Napier and Miller Ltd., Yoker, Glasgow; 1901, 4,647gt, 386 feet
T. 3-cyl. by Dunsmuir and Jackson Ltd., Glasgow.
Australind bought *Atholl* from James Warrack of Leith in 1919, and did not need to rename her as she fitted in with their naming scheme, whose only rule seemed to be that names should begin with a letter A. Australind sold her on in 1929, when she was bought by owners in Genoa who renamed her *Antonietta*. She was unwise enough to be at Norfolk, Virginia when Italy entered the Second World War in June 1940, and when the USA declared war, she was requisitioned by the US War Shipping Administration and put under the Panama flag as *Olambala*. She was one of the ships which were sunk to form part of Gooseberry Harbour No. 1 off Normandy in June 1944. *[Ian Farquhar collection]*

ARDENVOHR (lower)

William Denny and Brothers Ltd., Dumbarton; 1940, 5,025gt, 415 feet
Oil engine 4-cyl. 2SCSA by Barclay, Curle and Co. Ltd., Glasgow
Denny supplied Australind with their first motor ship in 1927, and company returned to the Dumbarton builder five times for repeats which gradually updated the design. *Ardenvohr* was the third, probably ordered before the Second World War broke out.

Here she is at anchor probably off New York on 23rd May 1942 at the end of her last completed voyage. At New York she loaded munitions, tanks and other military equipment for Australia, but never made it, thanks partly to the US Navy being totally unprepared for anti-submarine warfare, despite having watched what Great Britain had suffered for two and a half years. On 10th June, *Ardenvohr* was torpedoed by *U 68* in the sea lanes leading to the Panama Canal. The *U 68* encountered and sank three unescorted merchant ships that night. *Ardenvohr's* complement got away relatively lightly, only one man being lost, but the sinking must have been a repeat trauma for the 17 survivors of the *Velma Lykes* (2,572/1920) who had been taken on board when the US freighter had been torpedoed by *U 158* on 5th June

Australind were allowed to order a replacement from Dennys, a third *Australind* which emerged in 1944, and a near sister *Ashburton* was delivered from Dumbarton in 1946. *[Ian Farquhar collection]*

PHOTOGRAPHY MATTERS

Which ship?

Ian Farquhar has sent this fine photograph taken at Port Chalmers in the late 1880s. It is most likely an early charter to Tyser Line, and Ian lists four possibilities, all two-masted steamers known to have visited Port Chalmers in the period. Can any reader positively identify which ship it is, or eliminate any from the list below?

Ashleigh Brook	2,001/1883	W.G. Killick, London
Balmoral Castle	2,050/1876	J. Kilgour, London
Selembria	3,113/1882	R.M. Hudson, London
Worcester	2,908/1887	Great Western Steam Ship Co., Bristol

What yacht: *Record* 20

The request to identify the steam yacht in Royal Navy service on page 240 of *Record* 20 brought forth a number of interesting suggestions from readers. These included:

HMS *Sylvana,* built by Ailsa at Troon in 1907 for W.K. Millar, London as *Maid of Honour,* and served as a minesweeping yacht in the Second World War.

HMS *Rovenska,* built by Ramage and Ferguson in 1904 as the Austrian *Rovenska,* and after being seized served during the First World War as a boarding vessel. In 1920 she became Guglielmo Marconi's *Elettra,* the bows of which survive as a memorial to the wireless pioneer.

HMS *Dominica,* requisitioned in October 1939 and served as an examination vessel until laid up in 1944. She was built by Scotts of Greenock in 1905 as *Greta,* later becoming *Laranda, Dorothy* and *Devonia.*

These big steam yachts were well photographed, and many have appeared in books, including 'Steam Yachts' by David Couling and 'Salt Water Palaces'. Sadly, photographs of the three listed as civilian yachts fail to confirm the identification. Indeed, the closest is a photograph of HMS *Dominica* taken in 1947 and now with the World Ship Society, but this has many detailed differences.

Further consideration of the photograph in *Record* 20 suggests that it is a First World War view, with the yacht having heightened masts for wireless transmission. This would rule out HMS *Dominica* and HMS *Sylvana* which were not requisitioned during the First World War under any of their earlier names. With the First World War HMS *Rovenska* eliminated on grounds of appearance, we seem to

have drawn a blank, and further suggestions are welcome.

We would like to thank all those who wrote, or were subsequently sucked into this investigation, including John Bartlett, George Gardner, John B. Hill, Bill Lind, Phil Simons and Alexander McAusland. We are only sorry that their detective work has been, as yet, unrewarded by a solution.

Help put William Robertson on *Record*

Not a request for photographs, but for leads. One of the editors is well advanced with a work on William Robertson of Glasgow, a pioneer coastal steam ship owner well known for his so-called Gem Line. A very detailed fleet list has been compiled, and most photographs assembled, but what is conspicuously missing is any information on Robertson's family. If any reader can help, or can put us in contact with Robertson's successors (who sold out to Stephenson Clarke in the mid-1970s), we would be delighted to hear from them.

Catalogue of the Liverpool Street collection

The Great Eastern Railway Society has published a catalogue which lists all 1,887 negatives in the Liverpool Street Maritime Photographic Collection, now housed at the National Railway Museum, York. The negatives are mainly of British Railway's Eastern Region ships, with some Southern, Western, London Midland, and Scottish Region ships, and some British, Dutch, French and Belgian non-railway ships. The catalogue is available at £4.60 including postage from Ships in Focus.

Any clues?

Peter Poulter asks if anyone can help identify this vessel sunk in the entrance to Shoreham harbour.

EVERY PICTURE TELLS A STORY: AMSTERDAM   Martin Lindenborn

Even nowadays one can find interesting things on a junk market. Some time ago one of my friends found some glass negatives of views of the port of Amsterdam. One of these plates was still in a perfect condition and will be of interest for the readers. The photographer is unknown. The scene is the Oosterdok (East Dock), Amsterdam and the photograph can be dated to about 1900. Let us see what happens on the picture.

On the right side is the Dutch steamer *Ceres*. She belonged to the Koninklijke Nederlandsche Stoomboot Maatschappij (KNSM), one of the oldest Amsterdam steam shipping companies, established in 1856. *Ceres* was built in 1876 as yard number 24 of the Abercorn Shipbuilding Company, Paisley as *Phoebe* for C.J. Briggs, London. She was an awning-deck steamer of 1,013 tons gross and fitted with a compound engine of 500 IHP, constructed by J. and T. Young of Ayr. Possibly *Phoebe* was a speculation as Briggs had already sold her by 1877 to the KNSM, who renamed her *Ceres*. She had a long and practically eventless career with the new owners, most of the time in the liner service to the Mediterranean. Finally, in the autumn of 1906, she was sold for £2,400 to C. Martinolich e Figlio at Trieste, then in Austria-Hungary, and renamed *Flink*. Her end came on 26th of February 1911. On a voyage with a cargo of grape residue from Gallipoli to Ravigno she struck Merlera Rock, off Pola, and became a total loss.

Just ahead of the bow of *Ceres* a fine old barque is visible: *Prins Maurits Der Nederlanden*, a wooden corvette belonging to the Royal Dutch Navy. Once she was a beauty of 900 tons and 28 guns but, at the time the photo was taken, she was used as a guard-ship in the port of Amsterdam. Her keel was laid in June 1842 at the Naval Yard at Flushing and she was launched in 1849 as *Atalante*, after seven years on the stocks. But in the meantime a prince named Maurits was born and this was the reason that she was renamed when completed in 1850. Warfare at sea changed quickly in those days and already by 1869 she was paid off as completely obsolete, and

spent the rest of her long life as a guard vessel for training duties, firstly at Flushing and later in Amsterdam. The hulk was sold for demolition in 1905.

Further to the left is the *Sirius*, another KNSM-steamer, surrounded by river steamers and barges. At the time the photo was taken she was on the liner service to the East Prussian ports Stettin, Danzig and Königsberg. An important cargo from those ports to Amsterdam was flour in bags.

Sirius was another good old Scottish product, launched on 29th of September 1871 as yard number 149 by Scott and Co. of Greenock. A three-masted, flush-decked schooner of 597 tons gross, she had a compound engine of 400 IHP, constructed by the shipyard. She spent her 34 years' life under the KNSM flag without making history: a money earner for the owners. But her career became very interesting after being sold in the summer of 1905.

KNSM sold her to a Dutchman living in Paris, named L. Cornelissen and KNSM handed her over in the French Mediterranean port of Sète. Soon afterwards it became known what was the intention of her new owner. Mr. Cornelissen was operating as a representative of Caucasian rebels and, without renaming, she made between September 1905 and January 1906 an eventful voyage as a blockade runner with a cargo of weapons to the Black Sea. Very little is known about this part of her history, until 12th July 1906, when she again appeared in the shipping registers, now as *Katina*, flying the Greek flag, and owned by G.D. Andreadis of Piræus. During the Balkan War she was captured in October 1912 by the Turks and put into service for the Turkish Government, officially owned by Osmanli Seyr-i Sefain Idaresi of Istanbul. Her name remained *Katina*, but the flag became, of course, Turkish. War ended and she was given back in 1913 to Mr. Andreadis of Piræus, but not for a long period. On 11th July 1914 she hoisted the flag of Persia, and her name was changed to *Persepolis* and her home port became Bandar Abbas. She was owned by a Persian lady, Mrs. Anne Thrasybule Kirillou, living in

Istanbul, and some others, and G. Samothrakis of Piræus was appointed as manager. The old steamer was chartered by the Société Nationale de Grèce, Piræus and it was in service of that company that she was seized after a voyage from Piræus to Mersin and Iskenderun on 1st April 1915 in Iskenderun Roads by the French cruiser *D'Entrecasteaux* and sent to Port Said, being suspected of having a cargo of weapons on board. The French declared her a good prize and on 16th June 1915 she was placed under the French flag with the new name of *Ninive* and used as an auxiliary patrol vessel.

In April 1919 the French naval base at Saloniki became her new home but the old steamer was in such a bad condition that the French Navy decided to sell her. Indeed, on 30th June 1919 a Swiss citizen named Victor Besso, who lived in Istanbul, bought her but she remained under the French flag. He sold her shortly afterwards to Ch. Biliotti of Istanbul, who resold her in 1923 to Mrs. L. Joffredy. She appointed S.S. Psomiades & Co. as managers of the aged vessel, which was still named *Ninive* and was still flying the French flag. It is a pity that nothing is known about the end of this interesting steamer. In 1930 she was simply deleted from 'Lloyd's Register' with her existence being in doubt.

To revert to the photo, left of the *Sirius* one can see the so-called 'mastbok', the municipal sheer legs of Amsterdam, already in place by 1842. Amsterdam had at that time many shipyards, and they could hire the sheer legs when they had to place masts in new vessels or those under repair.

To the extreme left is a wooden tjalk. Dutch shipbuilders have constructed many hundreds of this type. Most were used for inland navigation but quite a lot were fitted for coastal trading, mostly to Baltic and North Sea ports, but they are known to have made voyages to the Mediterranean and even to South America.

(Many thanks to my friend Mr. Jochen Krüsmann of Goch, Germany for his indispensable help with the history of the *Sirius*)

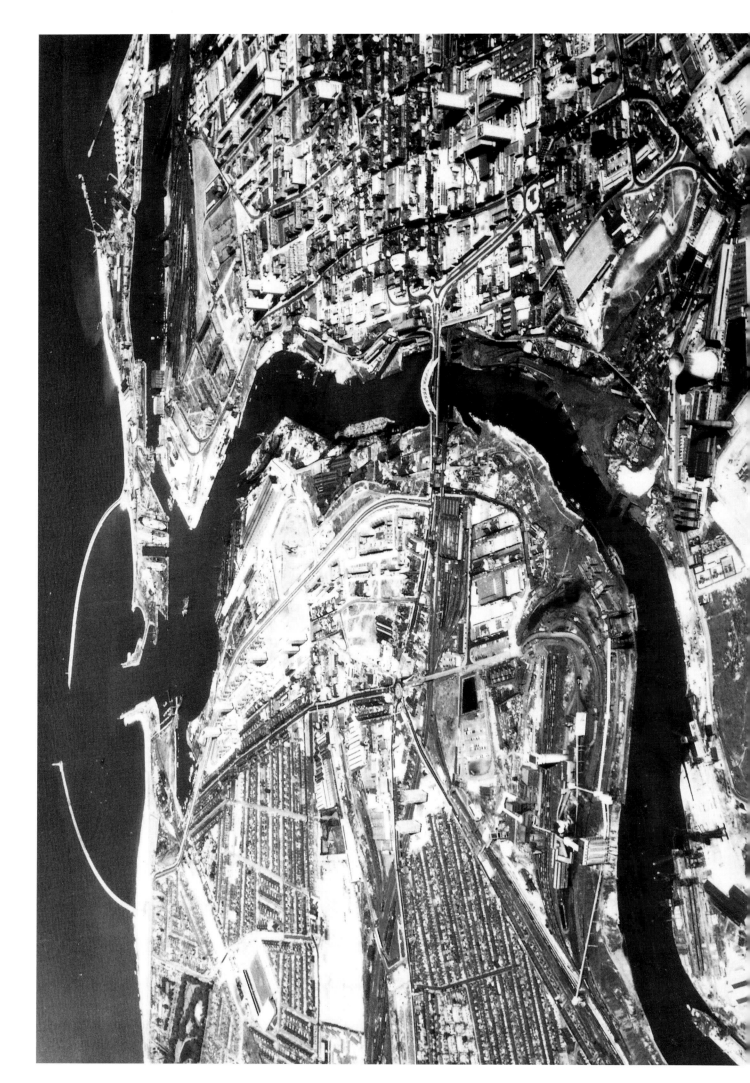

SUNDERLAND IN FOCUS 2 A second look back at the port and its ships.

John Lingwood

Sunderland in Focus 1 in Record 19 touched briefly on the origins of the port of Sunderland, examining its development as an outlet for the vast quantities of coal mined in the Durham Coalfield, and noted how, in earlier days, the 'Black Diamonds' were brought some six or seven miles down the River Wear from the collieries in flat-bottomed, 21-ton capacity, oar-propelled punts known as keels, to be transhipped into collier brigs and sloops moored in the harbour. These collieries marked the upper limit of commercial navigation for decades, albeit using only these tiny craft, however, by the nineteenth century, coal staithes, serviced by rail and suitable for much larger colliers, were operating successfully in the lower reaches of the river, and that upper navigational limit began to move downstream until, by the beginning of the Second World War, only an occasional cargo ship ventured as far as North and South Hylton, twin villages about five miles from the river mouth. Conveniently for our purposes, this five mile stretch of the River Wear can now be divided into three sections, which can be viewed from the Wearmouth, Queen Alexandra, and A19 (Hylton) road bridges. Using these as markers, 'then and now' aerial photographs can be compared to get some idea of how trade on the Wear has changed, and in many cases completely disappeared, over the years.

'Sunderland in Focus 1' offered a pictorial description of the activity within what was a highly successful, medium-sized port, prior to the decline of the coal trade and the closure, in the late 1980s, of the famous shipyards whose prodigious output over many years had justifiably earned for Sunderland the title 'the largest shipbuilding town in the world'. As was noted in that first article, much of this activity would have been visible from viewpoints at the east (downriver) side of the Wearmouth Bridge, the first of the bridges noted above. Unfortunately, a similarly interesting view to the west was blocked by the heavy structure of the adjacent railway bridge, whose girders allowed only glimpses of the shipping movements at the Lambton and Hetton coal staithes, on the south side of the river and only a stone's throw from the city centre. These staithes were, until nationalisation in 1947, owned by the vast Lambton, Hetton and Joicey Collieries (L.H. & J.C) group, and were

the outlet for their collieries, and at any one time, six or seven colliers, ranging in size from the tiny 150 deadweight vessels serving ports on the east-coast of Scotland, to the 4,500 tonners supplying the power stations and gas works of southern England, and worldwide export markets, might have been seen loading here.

The photograph opposite was taken in the mid-1960s, and clearly shows the lower stretch of the river, as featured in 'Sunderland In Focus 1', as well as the first half of the second section, now under review. By this time, coal shipments from the two river berths had ceased, although cargoes continued to be loaded in the South Docks, however, the spouts at the derelict Lambton and Hetton Staithes can still be identified in the photograph, on the right (south) side of the river, moving towards the bottom of the picture. The other loading point, Wearmouth Staithes, sited on the bend of the river opposite, was the outlet for the Wearmouth Coal Company, and was still operating, but despatching its product by rail and road, with its single loading spout used only by two self-propelled hoppers, Stephenson, Clarke's *Adderstone* and *Falstone*, which carried waste from Wearmouth Colliery, located immediately behind the staithes (but now demolished and the site of the Sunderland AFC football ground 'The Stadium of Light'), and Castletown Colliery a few miles upriver, to the North Sea for dumping. It is these two vessels which can be seen lying at the berth. Immediately upriver from Wearmouth Staithes on the north bank, was the location of MacColl and Pollock's engine works. Founded in 1894, this small establishment produced some 400 steam engines before closing in 1935. The stretch of river in front of the works, known as The Rack, provided the moorings used by colliers waiting their turn at Wearmouth.

As can be seen from the photograph, the river begins a large 'U-bend' above the staithes, and the enclosed land on the south bank was occupied by Sir James Laing's shipyard. Laings had operated from many sites on the Wear before settling here at Deptford where they quickly earned a worldwide reputation for building wooden-hulled, sailing, passenger and cargo liners. Progressing to composite construction, they delivered what is still regarded as the finest sailing ship ever built on the Wear, *Torrens*, of Joseph Conrad fame. Nearly sixty years of success were suddenly

followed by bankruptcy at the beginning of the 20th century, but a decision in 1909 to bring in Sir James Marr from J.L. Thompson's North Sands shipyard as manager, not only re-established the company, but sowed the seeds for the foundation of what later became known as the TLF group. This not only included J.L. Thompson, Laing, and Sunderland Forge, but encompassed many other local firms successful in the marine field. Eventually the group was to merge with the other Wearside giant, William Doxford, to form Sunderland Shipbuilders.

Until the Second World War, Laings launched their ships from both east and west sides of the 'U-bend' using berths facing up and down the river. After the war, the worldwide demand for larger vessels induced the company to close the west yard, using the land released to construct new fabrication shops and stockyards. The extent of this development, together with realigning and expanding the remaining down-river building berths, visible in the bottom left corner of the photograph, allowed Laings to build bulk carriers approaching 70,000dwt. Nowadays, the site continues its maritime connections as the UK construction base of the world-renowned materials handling company Liebherr Cranes. [*Author's collection*]

Left: a reminder of when coal was second only to shipbuilding on the Wear. The France, Fenwick collier *Clanwood* (2,180/1924) is drydocked in Austin's yard. This dates the view prior to 1938, when *Clanwood* was sold to German owners to become *Balkan*. Indeed, the date is likely May 1936, as the collier in the river is the Gas, Light and Coke Company's *Mr Therm* (2,974/1936), probably newly launched: she has no masts and note the tugs. Another Gas, Light and Coke steamer is docked beyond *Clanwood*, whilst in the river is a Cory collier.

the height of the depression, at a time when other owners were laying up, or selling off their ships in despair. Moored off the shipyard (furthest from the camera) is sister ship *Harmattan*, whilst ahead of her lies what is probably one of those many 'out of work' tramps. The photographs also show from varying angles, the Southwick engine works of George Clark, below the bridge on the north bank of the river. Founded about 1850, the company became part of the Richardsons, Westgarth Group in 1938, and a feature of the establishment was the 100-ton hammer head crane, seen here assisting the outfitting of a typical 10,000dwt tramp of the day, maybe one built at the adjacent William Pickersgill yard, tucked under the north west corner of the bridge.

The third section of the river is easily observed from the west (upriver) side of the Queen Alexandra Bridge, although this view is also restricted by a bend about a half-mile upstream. Fortunately, virtually everything of shipping note happened within that first half-mile. Since the 1970s it has also been possible to look back down the stretch of river above that bend, from our third marker, the A19 road bridge, positioned high above the twin villages of North and South Hylton. Incidentally, this might be a convenient point to mention that the sad reduction in Sunderland's maritime heritage over the past twenty years or so has brought one bonus, since it is now possible to walk (or cycle) almost uninterruptedly along the Coast to Coast Cycle Track from the tip of Roker Pier at the harbour mouth to the A19 bridge (and by way of this track, across to the west coast of England!) seeing all the points of interest noted in these two articles at close quarters.

These three consecutive aerial photographs actually give a false impression of the state of business in the yards in 1930. Looking downstream in the photograph on this page, the two ships under construction at Robert Thompson's shipyard belie the fact that the yard was soon to close forever, whilst above the bridge, the ship on the stocks at the, then, tiny yard of William Pickersgill (opposite page, left) had been built as a speculation in order to keep the workforce employed, and with no owner interested in purchasing her, was launched as the *Northwick* on 23rd September 1930, nominally for local shipowner James Westoll, part owner of the shipyard. Laid up for five years after completion, she was eventually sold, and made her maiden voyage as Ropner's *Alderpool* in 1936: the same year as the yard reopened following the depression.

A similar story was unfolding on the south side of the river, where Doxfords, internationally famous for the development of the Turret ship design in the last years of the nineteenth century, were also to close their gates for nearly

The second road bridge over the Wear, the Queen Alexandra, three miles upstream, was built in 1909 and links the districts of Deptford and Pallion on the south side, with Southwick. It is clearly shown in each of the three photographs on these two pages, taken in 1930, which together cover what was once a very busy section of the river. The bridge itself is something of an engineering masterpiece, consisting of a two-lane roadway built within a heavy girder structure carrying an upper deck supporting a rail track. Originally planned to link the collieries to the north and west of Sunderland with the Lambton, and South Dock staithes, the railway was, in fact, little used, and after only a short time was closed completely, leaving the structure to continue in use only as a road bridge to this day.

Looking back downstream, the second half of the second section of the river is in view, with the Southwick shipyard of Robert Thompson on the left side of the river (top right of the photograph on this page), and Laing's 'upriver' building berths just visible on the opposite bank.

The elder brother of Joseph Lowes Thompson who founded the more famous J.L. Thompson concern, Robert Thompson closed his small sideways-launching shipyard opposite Lambton Staithes, in order to concentrate on building larger ships at this Southwick yard, where the ship shown ready for launching is *Harmonic*, one of two sisters built by Thompson for J and C. Harrison in 1930. They were part of a huge order for 26 tramps in all, surprisingly ordered by the London company from various shipyards at

nearly four years shortly after these photographs were taken. Their Pallion shipyard was readily identified by the girders of the overhead, electric travelling crane installation which served the three berths of their east yard. Each individual crane in the system could originally lift some three tons, and could be used in combination with its neighbours for heavier lifts. It offered a distinct advantage over the traditional, virtually man-powered, pole derricks still in use in most British yards, and visible in the Pickersgill yard, and remained in use for nearly seventy years, until structural problems induced safety restrictions which progressively reduced their lifting capacity. The supporting uprights also imposed a beam limitation which was becoming unacceptable in terms of modern new

buildings, so the decision was taken in 1972 to clear the site and build a 'new shipyard' where modern technology allowed vessels to be built in a covered drydock. The two tankers lying at the fitting out quay are probably *Minister Wedel* and *Iron Chief*, part of a group of 10,000dwt vessels building for various Norwegian owners around 1930.

William Doxford and Sons Ltd. were also established marine engineers, and the extent of their combined premises can be seen from the right hand photograph on this page, with boundaries drawn by the Queen Alexandra Bridge at the top, a road running along the right-hand side, and another road running at right-angles to this down to the riverside, at the bottom of the picture. The marine engine works occupy the large buildings, centre

to bottom of the view, whilst to the left of these are the building berths of the west yard. Like Laings, Doxfords closed these down after the Second World War, not just to improve their shipbuilding facilities, but to also enlarge the engine works, because the company was by now a world market leader in marine engineering with their opposed-piston diesel engine. The development of this during the 1920s and 1930s played an important part in the success of the Doxford Economy Ship, a circa 9,000 deadweight cargo ship which the shipbuilding arm of the company introduced as the depression years ended, and which went on to form the basis of most of the cargo ship designs built by the yard over the next thirty years.

Part of the Doxford engine works can be seen in the middle of the left hand border of this photograph taken in 1979 and included to show the modernised Austin and Pickersgill shipyard, but also identifying, next door to the Doxford premises at Pallion, the site of two more shipyards. Short Brothers had laid down their yard in 1850 (on the site dominated left-top of the picture by two large mainly white rooved sheds). This closed after 114 years, following the delivery of its largest vessel, the 642-feet long, 24,710-deadweight bulk carrier *Carlton*. Their fitting out quay extended down river alongside Doxford's engine works, and was acquired, following this closure, by Bartram and Sons Ltd., whose shipyard, as recorded in 'Sunderland in Focus 1', was situated near the river mouth in the South Docks, and uniquely launched direct into the North Sea. As their newbuildings got larger in post-war years, they were unable to berth at their normal fitting-out quay, hence the purchase of Short's quay in 1964. Following the acquisition of Bartram by Austin and Pickersgill, the quay came under the latter's control with all 54 South Dock-built SD14s completed there. A Third Series example of that design is shown at the quay, with one of the later Fourth Series vessels fitting out, and two more building, across the river at Southwick.

56

Next to Shorts was the short-lived 'EGIS' shipyard, opened in 1918 by a syndicate comprising Ellerman, Gray, Inchcape and Strick. William Gray of Hartlepool managed the yard and caused great controversy in 1930 by announcing the closure of what was then regarded as the most modern shipyard in Britain. The yard was eventually sold in 1938 to local engineers, Steel and Co, who had recently taken on the construction of the ubiquitous Coles mobile crane. The large factory seen top left was constructed on the site to handle production of the various models introduced and, as demand increased, this was expanded upriver over the years, before extending downriver in 1964 into the white-roofed sheds (already mentioned) on the site of the now vacant Shorts Shipyard.

William Pickersgill had moved his shipyard from a position near the mouth of the river to Southwick about 1850, and his cramped premises remained pretty much unchanged (and as shown in the 1930 photograph on page 55) until 1954, with the opening of the 'Q.A' bridge in 1909 providing onlookers with a grandstand view of the art of ship building'. Next door to the Pickersgill shipyard was that of Sir John Priestman and Company, with the two premises separated by derelict land, and a large ballast hill, a throw-back to the days when ships would come to the river to load, ballasted with sand and gravel, which was then discharged as waste. Both the derelict land, and the ballast, were to play an important part in the nineteen fifties, when what was by then Austin and Pickersgill began the major re-development which resulted in the huge complex occupying most of photograph opposite. Before then, in 1943, William Pickersgill had extended their activities by taking over the Priestman yard, closed during the 'thirties depression, at the behest of the Admiralty who were desperately looking for additional berths on which to build frigates and escort vessels. After the war these berths were retained for commercial building, operating as Pickersgill's West Yard, alongside the original East Yard.

In 1954, the two companies, S.P. Austin (see 'Sunderland in Focus 1') and William Pickersgill were merged by their joint shareholders to form Austin and Pickersgill Ltd., and a massive reconstruction programme was begun at Southwick utilising the waste ground noted above, with site levelling employing material from the ballast hill. The photograph opposite shows how Pickersgill's old East yard was transformed into the fitting-out quay, with workshops and stores adjacent, whilst shipbuilding was centred on the realigned and lengthened 'Priestman' berths of the West Yard, refitted with modern cranage. At this time fabrication and assembly of steelwork was carried out in the dark-coloured sheds, centre right, but in 1975 the success of the company's SD14 and bulk carrier programmes induced a further expansion, and the additional light-coloured sheds nearer the river were added.

The major feature of this expansion, however, was the erection of a covered complex (top centre) containing 'one-and-a-half' building berths. As with the Pallion modernisation of a few years earlier, a new construction process was introduced, involving first commencing work on the aft-end of a newbuilding on a 'half-berth'. When this work had progressed sufficiently, the half-ship was moved across to the adjacent 'full berth' where the fore end was built-up on whilst work on another 'half-ship' began. The difference between the Pallion and Southwick processes was that, whilst building at the first named took place in a dry dock, which was then flooded to allow the half ship to be moved (and later floated out), at Southwick conventional slipways were fitted, with the half ship moved across using hydraulic rams and launching carried out in the traditional way.

This massive expansion of the A & P premises involved the site of one other shipyard. In 1912 Swan Hunter had commenced building from a yard next door to Priestman's which served mainly as an overflow site to their more famous river Tyne base, before it too fell victim of the Depression and was closed in 1933. Wartime emergencies brought about a reopening by the government-sponsored Shipbuilding Corporation Ltd. in 1943, and eleven standard cargo ships were built before closure again in 1947. After some years of occupation by a pipeline manufacturing company, Austin and Pickersgill acquired the site in the 1970s extension, and built the covered berth on the land.

The location of one other interesting, but short-lived, Sunderland shipyard is something of a mystery. This was the specialist yard laid down by Swan Hunter at the end of the First World War in response to a Government initiative for building reinforced concrete barges and tugs. Three tugs were completed by The Wear Concrete Building Co. Ltd. before the war ended and the programme was suspended, but whether the premises were positioned between Robert Thompson's shipyard and George Clark's engine works at Southwick, as some sources suggest or, as seems more likely, on land immediately next door to Swan Hunter's 'conventional' berths is open to question. Nothing remains at either site to help answer the question.

Today the village suburb of South Hylton has only two small anchors forming a feature on a landscaped river frontage to mark a maritime heritage dating back to the early nineteenth century, when it was the original location of the later-to-be world famous Doxford and Bartram shipbuilding companies. In more recent times, Wighams made ship's winches and steering gears here, and Forster's Forge manufactured the W.L. Byers patent stockless anchor, arguably the world-leader of its type for most of last century, together with countless stemframes and rudders fitted to ships built far and wide. The grassed leisure area now presented, also encompasses the site of the Ford Paper Mill, notable as the furthest upstream commercial berth on the river in recent times. Coasters bringing cargoes of raw materials were regular visitors here pre-war but, as with many things, the war brought changes which meant they rarely returned after the conflict. During the depression years, and again, briefly in the late 1950s, this otherwise redundant stretch of river above Pallion provided lay-up berths for a number of idle tramp ships, but now offers only a reminder of times past as the last resting place of the concrete tug Cretehawser. Built by the Wear Concrete Building Company in 1919, she was bought in 1935, along with a similarly constructed barge by the then River Wear Commissioners, to serve as a blockship to be used in the event of storm damage to coast defences. However, after the barge was sunk at her moorings by German bombers, it was thought prudent to tow Cretehawser to a safer berth upriver in case further enemy activity destroyed her in a position likely to present a hazard to shipping movements in the port.

So, it is now a positively rural view which is offered from the third of our bridges, a modern structure which carries the A19 trunk road over the river, and provides an opportunity to complete this second 'Sunderland in Focus' review. Looking downriver from the bridge, just one relic of the commercial past of this section of the Wear remains to be identified. Situated on the north bank just below the few houses and a pub (significantly named 'The Shipwrights Arms') which constitutes North Hylton, was Osbourne, Graham's shipyard, another long-gone victim of the Depression. Famous as builders of barques and full-rigged ships in their earlier days, they were restricted by the river width to building smaller tonnage in later years, but achieved some fame by their readiness to become involved with the construction of experimental ship designs such as the Monitor type, featuring corrugated sides, and the Ayre-Ballard 'arch type', notable for the inclusion of a 'reverse sheer', and an inward curve of the hull at deck level, aimed at providing a self-trimming facility for bulk cargoes. That they were selected by the Royal Navy to build a series of fast patrol vessels in Second World War, is surely an indication of the standard of work achieved at this yard, perhaps the least known of the many which each made their own contribution to Sunderland's proud claim to be 'The Largest Shipbuilding Town in the World' for most of the twentieth century.

Most colliery owners had a shipping connection of some sort: for LH & JC this had begun with the Earl of Durham's interests in 1853, but passed in 1919 to the Tanfield Steamship Company of Newcastle, which had Lord Joicey and his family, who now owned the collieries, as principal shareholders. Rarely owning more than five ships at a time,

the company operated mainly in the London trade during the winter, but moved some of its fleet into European and Mediterranean waters later in the year, from where they regularly returned home with Spanish and North African iron ore, esparto grass or Russian timber. Their vessels were amongst the largest on the coast, typified by *Harraton*,

built by S.P. Austin in 1930 at a cost of £45,000, and carrying some 4,300 tons. However, she only remained in the fleet for nine years before being sold to French owners at a profit of £10,000 in February 1939. [*Frank & Sons, South Shields; Author's collection*].

Some idea of the number of ships using the Lambton and Hetton staithes can be gauged from the fact that LH & JC ran their own fleet of four (later reduced to three) paddle tugs from 1858 expressly to handle them. *Eppleton Hall* (166/14), once of this fleet, was destined to become its most famous unit following rescue from the scrap yard in 1969 by Scott Newhall, who subsequently sailed her to San Francisco in 1969/1970, where she remains to this day as an exhibit at the US port's Maritime Museum. Her smaller consort *Houghton* (133/04) is pictured here passing J.L. Thompson's North Sands shipyard, but wearing the funnel colours of France, Fenwick Tyne and Wear Co. Ltd., following that company's acquisition *en-bloc* in 1945 of the Lambton vessels, prior to the nationalisation of the British coal industry. Before this the fleet carried the 'three red bands' insignia, as shown in the photograph of *Harraton*, said to be a reference to local poem/folk song (The Lambton Worm) which commemorates the brave deed of an early Lord Lambton who returned from the Crusades to slay a 'dragon' which had been terrorising the local villagers, by cutting it into 'three halves'.

By dint of various acquisitions and amalgamations during the first half of last century, France, Fenwick Tyne and Wear became the largest tug operator on the rivers Tyne and Wear, and a direct line can still be traced to the current main contractor on the rivers. However, like the Lambton tugs, its origins lay firmly with the coal industry through the Fenwick and Stobart families who were the fitters (sales agents) for the Wearmouth Coal Company, and the co-founders of the William France, Fenwick collier fleet. *[A. Duncan: late F. Ypey/Author's collection]*

It was a combination of circumstances which forced the closure of Robert Thompson's shipyard in 1933. The 1930s depression was the prime cause, and it was undoubtedly because of this that the yard had to look outside its traditional tramp-ship market for new work: its efforts eventually bringing in orders for two refrigerated trawlers, claimed at the time to be the largest in the world. Unfortunately, before they were completed in 1932, their Portuguese owners were declared bankrupt, leaving Thompsons with two highly specialist vessels, launched as *Corte Real* and *Descobridor*, on their hands. To compound the builder's problems the sole director, Errol Thompson, grandson of the founder of the company, died suddenly in 1932 and the following year the firm went into voluntary liquidation. It was not until May 1933 that the trawlers were sold, very much below their original contract price of £45,000, to French owners based in Fecamp, taking the names of *Le Jacques Couer* and *Le Dougay-Trouin*. Both vessels served their new owner Compagnie Generale de Grand Peche, fishing waters between Newfoundland and the White Sea, until the war. The subsequent history of the former vessel (pictured) is confused since there was more than one *Le Jacques Couer* based in Fecamp at that time. One report suggests she was sunk by German forces at Dunkirk on the 21st May 1940, alternatively, it is claimed that she served in the German Navy as submarine hunter *UJ 2205* until April 1943 when she was lost in the Mediterranean. Her sister's history is somewhat clearer, with indications that she was working out of Port de Bouc in 1942 and Casablanca in 1944, followed by service in the French Navy until 1945 after which she returned to Fecamp and fishing off Newfoundland. From 1964 she was owned in Greece, and was still recorded in the Greek Register in 1988 under the name *Poseidon*. *[late F. Ypey; Author's collection]*.

Above: Seen just after launch from the Southwick yard of Swan, Hunter and Wigham Richardson is *Forestash* (1,500/1924), on 17th April 1924. The self-trimming collier was part of the ambitious post-war expansion plans of Glasgow coaster owners Mann, Macneal, but which led the company into bankruptcy in 1926. *Forestash* then had a variety of names: *Cramlington*, the Finnish *Herbert*, and the British *Morar*, as which she was mined off Harwich on 26th November 1943.

To the right can be seen the *Stottpool*, another victim of the depression which set in after the First World War. Launched shortly before *Forestash*, she was the only ship built for the Stottpool Steamship Co. Ltd. managed by T.B. Stott of Liverpool. She never traded for them, and in December 1925 was repossessed by Swan, Hunter. They sold her to Norwegian owners who renamed her *Nidareid*. In 1946 she was sold to China as *Way Tung*, and in 1950 found herself in the Hong Kong-based fleet of Wallem and Co., who put her under the Panama flag as *Nidar*, trading mainly between Bangkok and Hong Kong with rice. She was broken up in 1954. The splendid paddle tug is tentatively identified as James Irwing's *Agamemnon* (129/1872), but confirmation would be appreciated. *Ian Rae collection]*

Opposite bottom: One trade which did manage to continue during the Depression, albeit on a reduced scale, was the east-coast coal trade, and newbuilding contracts continued to be placed from time to time. For the traditional collier building yards, however, competition for these orders was increased as those builders whose berths were normally filled by larger ships had to look elsewhere for work. Thus we find 'big' names like Hawthorn, Leslie, Vickers and Laing delivering vessels into the coal trade, no doubt at low prices, in an attempt to keep their yards open. Typical of Swan, Hunter's contribution to this market was the *Flathouse* (1,546/1931), built for Stephenson Clarke especially to supply Portsmouth gas works, a task she fulfilled - with occasional diversions to other customers - for the next thirty years. The allocation of this order to their Sunderland shipyard was, perhaps, a last attempt to stave off the inevitable. Sadly, it failed, and the yard closed down after *Flathouse* was delivered. [*A. Duncan; the late F. Ypey/Author's collection*].

This page top: This photograph was taken in September 1995 from a position very near to the south-west corner of the Wearmouth Bridge, with a landscaped Lambton and Hetton staithes in the foreground, and the remaining buildings of Wearmouth staithes on the knuckle opposite. The sheds in the centre background are the former fabrication and assembly shops of Laing's shipyard, and to their right, across the river, is roughly the site of Robert Thompson's Southwick shipyard. As already noted, the Laings' yard is now owned by Liebherr Cranes and the structure in the centre of the photograph is one of a pair of gantry cranes completed at their premises for fitting on board a Gearbulk bulk carrier building in China. In all some six ship-sets of these cranes were completed at the yard, with delivery involving hiring a Bugsier heavy-lift crane to transfer the gantries on to a barge which was towed downriver to the Corporation Quay (see 'Sunderland in Focus 1'). Here the first ship-sets were lifted on to a heavy-lift cargo ship which carried them to China for installation. After two such trips the operation was simplified by bringing subsequent bulkers to Sunderland: the cranes still needed to be barged downriver, but they were then installed directly on board ship. [*J. Dobson*].

This page bottom: *Blue Galleon* (712/1924) was typical of many intermediate-sized coasters of around 900dwt which were regular callers at Sunderland. Equally at home in the Scottish or Thames/South Coast coal trades, they were also handy-sized for working to the Continent. When bombed and sunk off Hammond Knoll on the 15th November 1940 she was carrying cement from London to Sunderland, a trade which frequently provided satisfactory backhaul employment for her, and many other vessels of her type. Built by Cochrane and Sons Ltd. at Selby, *Blue Galleon* was owned in Newcastle-upon-Tyne by the Galleon Shipping Co. Ltd. (Heslop and Robson, managers) and occasionally took cargoes to the upriver berth of Ford Paper Mills. [*Roy Fenton collection*]

61

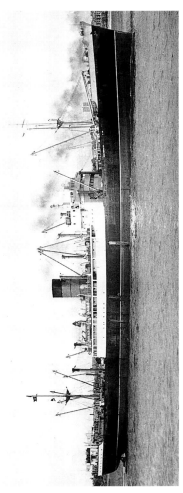

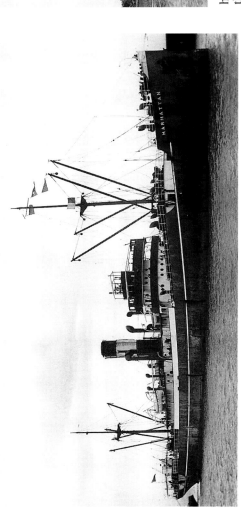

Above left: Robert Thompson's *Harmattan* (4,558/1930) featured the poop, long-bridge and forecastle layout which was arguably that most favoured by British tramp ship owners, prior to the 'design revolution' of the 'thirties. This period saw the introduction of many 'economy' designs, almost all of which featured the open shelter deck configuration, along with such refinements as cruiser sterns, raked stems and 'streamlined' superstructures, all aimed at improving operating efficiency. After a long career, latterly as *Marga*, she was broken up at Split in 1971. *[World Ship Photo Library]*

Below left: Though not as prolific as Harrison, Glasgow owner Hugh Hogarth was another who felt able to add new tonnage to its fleet throughout the depression years with *Baron Elphinstone* (4,635/1937) one of a pair of 8,888 deadweight open shelter deckers delivered by Sir James Laing. The launch of this vessel on the 18th September 1937 could be said to

have marked the beginnings of your author's career as a shipping writer, since he was taken that day by his father to Lambton Staithes where he worked, and from the deck of the LH&JC tug *Houghton*, moored just below the shipyard, watched the vessel enter the water. The treat ended with a ride on the footplate of a saddle-tank shunter at the staithes, and permission to blow the whistle! The experience just had to be put down on paper and submitted to the children's page of a local newspaper, who kindly published it and rewarded the effort with the prize of an adventure storybook. *[Roy Fenton collection]*

Above right: Much of Laing's wartime output, like that of sister yard J.L. Thompson, was devoted to the building of standard design oil tankers, so the winning of a prestigious contract for two intermediate class cargo liners for Cunard immediately after the war was certainly a feather in their cap. *Arabia* (8,723/1947) was the second vessel of this pair, remaining in the fleet until 1963. *[Roy Fenton collection]*

Opposite, bottom right: Another launch with personal memories was that of *Hylton* (5,197/1936), which I watched from the opposite bank on the 31st October. Built for the Hebburn Steam Ship Co. Ltd. of Newcastle-upon-Tyne under the 'Scrap and Build' programme she was, at the time, the largest vessel to be built by William Pickersgill. Her nominal owner, Sir William Souter, was born in Sheffield and named his main company and its ships after the River Sheaf of that city. Later he spent some time on Wearside at South Hylton, hence the choice of name for this new ship, sadly lost in 1941 from a homeward bound Atlantic convoy. *Sheaf* had already sampled diesel propulsion in 1929 with *Sheaf Holme* (4,811/1929), also built by Pickersgill. so it was no surprise to see the choice continued with *Hylton*, however, unlike that earlier ship. and most other thirties-built motor ships which were fitted with Doxford machinery, this new delivery featured a North Eastern Marine diesel of 2,110 BHP. NEM did not pursue construction of their own engine but instead opted (like many other engine builders worldwide) to build the Doxford design under licence. [*A. Duncan*]

This page top: The Shipbuilding Corporation yard at Southwick was managed during its short life by J.L. Thompson and relied heavily on their resources for its operation. *Benvannoch* (7,087/1944) was a standard Type 'D' tramp ship launched as *Empire Tudor*. Acquired in 1948 by London-Greek Goulandris Brothers she sailed as *Grandyke* before joining the Ben Line fleet in 1949 for seven years. She became *Medina Princess* in 1956, ending her career six years later when she grounded on a reef near Djibouti. [*F.R. Sherlock*]

Middle: The Priestman yard at Southwick was, perhaps, unique, in that it was owned and operated by one man throughout its life. Laid down in 1883 by John (later Sir John) Priestman, it launched its last ship 50 years later, known only by its builder's number 299. It was not until 1937 that the vessel was purchased by Öivind Lorentzen, Oslo as *Rio Novo* and the yard officially closed. Seen here in what appears to be early Second World War neutrality markings, *Rio Novo* survived the war, and in 1949 was converted to what must have been one of the very earliest liquefied gas carriers, the *Ultragaz*. Later names were *Gasbras Sul* and *Mundogas Sul*. She was laid up at Rio de Janeiro in December 1963, and broken up locally early in 1967.

Priestman was a County Durham farmer's son who worked in the drawing office at Blumer's yard before becoming Chief Draughtsman for William Pickersgill. From his own yard, and investments in collieries and shipping he amassed a personal fortune, much of which was donated to build churches and colleges, and to the setting up of many charities benefiting the poor. [*F.W. Hawks, George Scott collection*]

Bottom: In its relatively short history the Newport-based shipowner Pardoe-Thomas and Co. Ltd, experienced considerable success but, with hindsight and like many of its contemporaries, it could be said to have imprudently engaged in a massive newbuilding programme in the late 'twenties which added eight ships to its fleet, but contributed greatly to its premature demise. Three of these ships came from Priestman's shipyard, with *Knight of the Rose* (3,865/1929) the second of the trio. Unusually for the day, these vessels were 'tween deckers designed for the liner trade, and gained a decidedly modern look from their squat, raked funnel and raked masts. Pardoe-Thomas did not keep her long; in 1933 she was sold to United Africa as *Gambian*, and in 1936 to Scindia Steam Navigation Co. Ltd. as *Jalamani*. She remained in this Bombay-based fleet until 1955, and then carried the names *Athos* and *Filia* until broken up in Italy in 1964. [*A.Duncan, George Scott collection*]

'Monitor' corrugated hull form, with the latter built with a traditional, flat-sided hull. The experiment, aimed at proving by practical comparison the claims of improved efficiency made for the Monitor design, was inconclusive but, undeterred, the company later became involved in the construction of *Arcwear* (4,157/1934), one of three vessels built to demonstrate the merits of Sir Joseph Isherwood's Arcform hull design (see *Record* 1, pages 52 and 53). This proved to be a much more satisfactory exercise, and in the late 'thirties Shorts built several more vessels incorporating Isherwood's ideas. Amongst these were three vessels for the London-Greek Rethymnis and Kulukundis group, the last of the trio being *Elias G. Kulukundis* (5,500/1938). She lasted well, for a steamer, not being sold until 1960 when she became *Mariannina* and later *Raffaela*, going for scrap only in 1970. [*George Scott collection*]

Left: *Thetis* (4,123/1930) was another vessel delivered to the R & K stable, in this case for the ownership of the Nereus Steam Navigation Co. Ltd., managed in London by Hadjilias and Co. Ltd. She was the last of only 34 ships built by the EGIS yard during its ten years of active life, and like all the others she was constructed with a William Gray builder's number (1037). *Thetis* was sold to Spanish owners in 1955, and registered in Panama as *Ely*. She foundered in Dunkirk roads on 1st February 1959 after being damaged in a collision in fog. [*George Scott collection*]

Above left: Not all Wear shipyards in the inter-war years had the luxury of an 'in-house' design office, nevertheless those in this position were generally not averse to involvement with new ideas produced by outside consultants. In 1925, for instance, Shorts built two sister ships, *Newbrough* and *Simonburn*, for Common Brothers, the former incorporating the

Above right: Mention has been made in the text of the significant parallel development by William Doxford of their opposed piston diesel engine and the 'Economy' class cargo vessel. Seen here when almost new on 4th May 1935, *Sutherland* (4,956/1935) was the prototype of this design which, with continuous improvement and increases in size, was the mainstay of Doxford's cargo ship production for many years. *Sutherland* was sold in 1936 and as *British Prince* was sunk by the Luftwaffe off Spurn Point on 26th September 1941. [*J. and M. Clarkson*]